Family Writes

Also by Peggy Epstein

Great Ideas for Grandkids (McGraw Hill, 2003)

Capital Ideas for Parents

Father's Milk by Andre Stein, Ph.D. with Peter Samu, MD

The Golden Rules of Parenting by Rita Boothby

A Grandmother's Guide to Babysitting by Ruth Meyer Brown

How to Avoid the Mommy Trap by Julie Shields

The Man Who Would Be Dad by Hogan Hilling

Save 25% when you order any of these and other fine Capital titles from our Web site: *www.capital-books.com*.

Family Writes

Parenting with Pens, Pencils and PCs

Joel Epstein, Ph.D. and Peggy Epstein

Capital Ideas for Parents

CAPITAL
BOOKS, INC.
Sterling, Virginia

Capital Books, Inc.
P.O. Box 605
Herndon, Virginia 20172-0605

ISBN 1-933102-06-3 (alk.paper)

Library of Congress Cataloging-in-Publication Data
Epstein, Joel, 1964-
  Family writes : parenting with pens, pencils and PC's / Joel Epstein
and Peggy Epstein.
      p. cm.
  Includes bibliographical references.
  ISBN 1-933102-06-3 (pbk. : alk. paper)
  1. Communication in the family. 2. Parenting. 3. English language--
Composition and exercises. 4. Creative activities and seat work.
I. Epstein, Peggy. II. Title.

  HQ518.E665 2005
  649'.51--dc22

                                                            2005019602

Printed in the United States of America on acid-free paper that meets the American National Standards Institute Z39-48 Standard.

First Edition

10 9 8 7 6 5 4 3 2 1

Contents

Introduction: You Want Me to Do WHAT with My Kids 1

Chapter 1: Celebrate with Words. 7

New Year's Day. 8

The Prediction Jar 8

Letters to Yourself. 10

Valentine's Day 11

Pair a Treat with a Valentine Message 11

Puzzle Your Valentine 12

Mother's Day or Father's Day 14

Two-Way Scrolls. 14

Giant Personalized Crossword Puzzle. 15

Make a Memory Book. 16

Fourth of July 17

Personal Declaration of Independence. 17

Sidewalk Story 18

Thanksgiving 19

Little Baskets of Thanks 19

The Thanksgiving Extravaganza 20

Round-Robin Thanksgiving Messages 21

Chapter 2: It's All About Me! 23

The Toddler as Writer 24

Official Birthday Writing Sample 25

The Giant Birthday Book 26

Journals, Journals, and More Journals 27

Add-Me-Up Autobiography 29

Hairography 30

Pseudonyms, Serious and Silly 31

Personal Profile Sheet 32

I Used to…But Now I… 33

Thank-You Notes 34

Chapter 3: **A Family of Wordsmiths** **37**

Communication Tag 38

Two-Way Journals 39

Hypothetical Questions 40

Wow! That's some Good Advice 41

Age "Poems" 42

Writer-of-the-Month 44

"I See, You See" 45

Family Ad Campaign 46

Today's Top Ten List 47

Vacation Journals 48

Family Newsletters 49

The Multi-Caption Photo Adventure 51

Family Trivia Board Game 52

Family History 53

Chapter 4: **Take a Bite . . . Stop and Write.** **55**

Munching Memories 56

Food Fight 57

Neighborhood Recipe Book 58

Raving Restaurant Reviews 60

Become a Family of Consumer Watchdogs 62

How to Make a PBJ 63

The Great, Never-Ending Chili Experiment 64

Guess What I Just Ate! 65

Eat Your Words 66

Menu Mania (version 1) 67

Menu Mania (version 2) 68

Chapter 5: **Pages and Pages of . . . Sports Pages** **69**

"Fan"tastic Fan Mail 71

Around the Diamond 73

The Ultimate, Incredible Dream Play .75

Play-by-Play by You 76

Invent-a-Sport 77

Super Sports Journals 78

What a Good Sport! 79

Astounding Stories of Super Sports Heroes 80

Prepositional Plays 81

Become Experts on a Little-Known Sport 82

Chapter 6: **Just for Fun . . . Designing Your Own Activities** **83**

Compromise Island 85

Write Short 88

Cut-Up Communication 90

Pen-Pal Package Deal 91

Nursing Home Narrations 92

Party Plans 94

Pre "Historic" Writing Party 96

And a Final Idea: Find Out More about
Writing and Writers 97

Chapter 7: **The Right Writer Writes Right . . . er, Make that Correctly** **99**

And Parts of Speech Are Important Why? 101

Norbert the Noun Nerd 101

Prepositional Pigs 102

Super Bowl Special: Adjectives vs. Adverbs 103

Vivid Verbs 105

Who Invented Punctuation Anyway?. 106

    How Does This End? 106

    Quotation of the Day 107

    Comma Confusion 108

    It's (or is it "Its?") True: Apostrophes May Disappear. . . 110

    Organize That! 112

    The Imaginary Toy Shelf. 112

    Put THIS in Order! 113

    Organization: Challenge Level. 114

    Syl-lab-i-ca-tion 116

Epilogue 117

You Want Me to WHAT with My Kids?

• •

SCENE: *A woman sits at a computer. A man sits next to her. They gaze at the screen intently for several moments. Then the woman throws her hands up in the air, palms upward.*

Peggy: Ta da! So what do you think?

Joel: I think it'll be great when we're done.

Peggy: But we *are* done. Right there—that's the last word in the last chapter.

Joel: Sorry, Mom. We're not done.

Peggy: Well, if you think we need to include more activities, I can—

Joel: Actually, I think we've included plenty of activities.

Peggy: So what's missing?

Joel: Motivation.

Peggy: Motivation? And to think it was my idea to write this book with my son, the psychologist.

Joel: Just think about it, Mom. Most families are so busy they don't even eat dinner together. What makes you think they'll find time in their hectic schedules to *write* together?

Peggy: Well, because, we've come up with all these fun writing activities.

Joel: Ugh! You still don't get it. Okay, let's say I've flipped through this book. And let's say I even think my family might enjoy some of these activities. I'm still not really motivated to actually do them. In fact, I could probably come up with a million reasons *not* to do them.

Peggy: A million?

Joel: Okay, not a million. But really, think about it. Families get stuck in routines that are hard to break. Starting a new routine is ridiculously difficult.

Peggy: You're exaggerating again. Look at the Meyers. Just last year they started going to that Thursday night bowling league. They've been at it non-stop.

Joel: But they had *motivation.*

Peggy: Meaning?

Joel: Ever since they had Becky's birthday party at the lanes, she's been obsessed with trying to match her uncle's top score of 202. They've made bowling into something the whole family can share.

Peggy: So we can just tell other families that instead of bowling, they can write together.

Joel: Right . . .

Peggy: Why *do* you always have to be so sarcastic? I'm serious.

Joel: I know you're serious. And I think there are some great ideas in here. But I'm also serious about the idea that families simply aren't going to do any of them unless we give them plenty of reasons.

Peggy: How can we do that?

Joel: By explaining why participating in the activities is a good idea.

Peggy: Well, like I said, they're fun.

Joel: That's a start, but we need more than that.

Peggy: How about this? A family that writes together is a family that increases the amount, and quality, of their communication.

Joel: Okay. That's good, but why would a family want to do that?

Peggy: Argh! You're such a psychologist. It's good when families communicate.

Joel: I agree. But why?

Peggy: Well, so they can express their feelings to one another, so they can resolve conflict easier, so they can grow closer to one another, so they get to know each other better—

Joel: And you're saying that these exercises will do all that?

Peggy: *(hesitantly)* Sure.

Joel: Cool. So why else would parents want their family to do any of these things we've written about?

Peggy: You mean there needs to be more?

Joel: It wouldn't hurt . . .

Peggy: I'm stumped.

Joel: Okay. Let me at this for a while. *(He leans over the keyboard and starts typing.)* We should explain that this is really no big deal.

Peggy: What do you mean, "no big deal?"

Joel: *(frantically typing)* It's like this. If a parent tries to make a big deal about trying these things, kids are sure to freak out and be resistant.

Peggy: You mean sort of like when I made that kidney pie for dinner?

Joel: You just won't let that go, will you? But yes. If you make a big deal out of what a cool thing something is, kids are sure to hate it. Parents have to be a bit sneaky.

Peggy: I thought you were all about open and honest communication?

Joel: I am. But there's a way to do it.

Peggy: And how's that?

Joel: For example, maybe parents could suggest one of the activities when they hear that all too familiar, "I'm bored . . ."

Peggy: Or during a long car ride.

Joel: Or when they're waiting for the pizza to be delivered.

Peggy: That's excellent. Some of these quickie activities just take five or ten minutes. Maybe they can even do one instead of "just-one-more-story-before-bed."

Joel: Or to break the monotony of a boring family get-together.

Peggy: Geez, Joel. You're such a grump.

Joel: No really, I'm serious. That would be great. Instead of having to sit around listening to Aunt Josephine complain all afternoon, we could all do one of these activities.

Peggy: You've got a point. I could see us doing "Legal Graffiti" or an "Add-Me-Up Autobiography."

Joel: I think doing a "Multiple-Caption Photo Adventure" with Uncle Jack would be a hoot.

Peggy: He'd never do it.

Joel: Why not?

Peggy: Because even though he's really smart, he's self-conscious about never finishing high school. He'd make some excuse. Like his arthritis is bothering him. But really, he wouldn't want anyone to see that he can't spell.

Joel: Perfect!

Peggy: Now what are you talking about?

Joel: You've just identified another reason why people may never use any of the ideas we've written about. They just don't have enough self-confidence in their own writing skills. You don't know how many times I've heard people say, "I don't like to write," or "I hated English," and even "I don't know what I'd do without my computer's spell-checker."

Peggy: You don't have to be an NBA superstar to go out and shoot a few hoops with your kids.

Joel: Um . . . I think you're mixing metaphors here, Mom.

Peggy: That's exactly my point! Here, let me do this part. *(She takes over the keyboard)*. The fun of shooting hoops is not sinking every basket, but simply playing together.

Joel: Okay . . .

Peggy: Look at it like this. The whole thing isn't about grammar and spelling; it's about ideas—the writing is really in the thinking and talking you do together, not in the mechanical act of putting the words on paper or on a computer screen. For both parents and kids, getting hung up on stuff like handwriting, grammar, or spelling—that won't just dampen enthusiasm, it'll wash it away in a tidal wave!

Joel: So you're saying it's OK if the writing is full of grammatical errors?

Peggy: Sort of like that sentence? Sure. Like I said, these activities are not really about the writing, they're about sharing ideas. But nevertheless, doing them more and more will help improve kids' skill levels and help them gain confidence in their written words.

Joel: Another benefit!

Peggy: So now we're done?

Joel: No. You've got the parents sold. Now you've got to sell it to the kids. Writing is just too geeky for most kids.

Peggy: I disagree. Kids don't have to be convinced. First of all, most of them love making up stories, and it's also something lots of kids do every day—

Joel: Yeah, but in school it's different because—

Peggy: No, not at school. At home. On the computer. Think about chat rooms. What are kids doing in chat rooms?

Joel: They're writing.

Peggy: Exactly.

Joel: And they're having fun writing.

Peggy: Right. So I think for today's kids there's already a connection between "writing" and "fun." But more than that, I think that whenever parents offer undivided, enthusiastic attention, whether an activity involves a basketball or a pencil and paper, kids think "fun."

Joel: And I guess we know it works.

Peggy: Why do you say that?

Joel: Because we just did it. We wrote together.

Chapter 1

Celebrate with Words

· ·

Peggy: I think we should begin this chapter with a checklist of things people need for the holidays and end the list with "lots of pencils and plenty of paper."

Joel: And that's exactly why I hate holidays.

Peggy: Oh really? I just thought you were a grouch.

Joel: No, I'm serious about this one. I feel stressed just thinking about "holiday checklists." And I'm not alone. Holidays can be one of the most stressful times in a person's life.

Peggy: I know that's true, but I feel so sad for those people. Holidays have always been such joyous occasions for our family. I just love watching people open the presents I've carefully selected. And it's so fun getting to see Aunt Liz and Uncle Louie—we hardly ever get to see them.

Joel: And you really think all the commotion associated with the holidays would make for a good time to do a writing project?

Peggy: Absolutely. We're not just talking about the big holiday rush during December, but holidays throughout the year. Like Independence Day and Valentine's Day.

Joel: I know. And Mother's Day, too.

Peggy: Thanks for remembering.

Joel: Well, that's what these activities are really good for—creating lasting memories.

Peggy: But not only that, they're a chance for families to share time together. And they don't have to do everything we say word-for-word. They can modify them to fit their own lifestyles, to start their own family traditions.

New Year's Day

The Prediction Jar

Gain some insight into your children's thoughts by seeing what they have to say about the future. Share your ideas about the coming year as well.

1. Provide everyone with a preprinted sheet on which participants will pencil in their predictions for the New Year. You might want to make the list personal (predictions about the family) or general—or a combination of both. Here are some examples to get you started:

   Which member of the family will grow the most? _____

   How many pennies will there be in the penny jug by the end of next year? _____

   How much snow will fall this year? _____

   On what day will we have the hottest summer temperature, and what will it be? _____

   What will be the farthest any family member will travel? ____

   Who will be elected President? _____

   Who will win the Super Bowl, World Series, etc.? _____

   Instead of printed sheets, you may want to create a template on the computer that everyone can access. Simply take turns filling in your own responses, print, and clear. Encourage family members to dream up any other predictions they wish and add them to the list.

2. Fold up the prediction sheets and stuff them into a large empty jar. Glue the lid on. On top of the lid write, "Do not open until January 1st _____." You might like to keep the jar in a visible spot throughout the year, or you may want to tuck it away until the special moment.

3. Make a ritual of smashing the jar on New Year's Day—put it in a grocery carton before you shatter it with a hammer. (Obviously, grown-ups should lift out the papers and shake off any glass slivers.)

Note: If you're skeptical about this step, you could simply store the predictions in a box—but that takes away a lot of the drama!

4. Spend some time discussing the predictions and then repeat the process for the following year.

Letters to Yourselves

1. On New Year's Day, start a yearly ritual: provide everyone with a few sheets of nice writing paper, a matching envelope, and a new pen.

2. Invite everyone to write letters to themselves, listing goals they would like to accomplish in the New Year. Make sure everyone knows each letter will be sealed individually (using tons of tape*) and stored until the following New Year's Day.

    *VITAL: Everyone must rest assured that a letter will only be read by its own writer.

    Some tips:

    - You might want to precede the activity with a few examples to keep kids from setting themselves up: for example, a daughter who might write that in the coming year she hopes to learn to ride her own horse (which she doesn't—or will not—own) might be encouraged to write instead, "try horseback riding." You might remind everyone that "winning the lottery" is really a wish rather than a goal. In other words, encourage the realistically attainable.
    - Suggest writers state goals positively: "Keep remembering to do homework" rather than "Don't forget to do homework."
    - Propose that perhaps at least one goal somehow addresses the topic of relationships to others by suggesting a whole range of diverse subjects: reducing squabbles, remembering birthdays, demonstrating sympathy, etc.

3. Explain that all family members will seal their own individual envelopes with tape, write over the tape, etc. so that the envelopes will be tamperproof. Or—more dramatically—use sealing wax! This way, writers will be able to write more freely, confident in their privacy.

4. Distribute letters 365 days later on the following New Year's Day. Respect decisions about sharing the content of last year's letter; while some family members may be eager to read aloud and discuss their entire letters, others may not care to share at all.

Note: Composing and printing out letters using a computer may provide an attractive alternative to some, although you might point out to kids that they might enjoy comparing last year's handwriting to this year's.

Valentine's Day

Pair a Treat with a Valentine Message

As a family, create a "puns + goodie" package and then surprise friends and relatives. Some examples follow, but encourage everybody to come up with original ones if they can.

For a starting point, check out a batch of joke and riddle books from the library and see what kind of ideas you find. You'll have fun brainstorming—an important ingredient in the learning-to-write process. And don't be afraid to be corny or to let kids express sentiments that are less than lovable.

Examples:

- A hand-polished apple (or an entire bushel!). Message: "You're the apple of my eye" *OR* "Guess how big the worm is!"

- A freshly-baked strawberry tart (or an entire pie!) or some chocolate-dipped strawberries. Message: "I love you berry much" *OR* "You're berry . . . (whatever's appropriate)."

- A basket heaped with cashews, pecans, or pistachios. Message: "I'm nuts about you" *OR* "You're nuts but I like you anyway."

- An assortment of teas in a pretty teacup. Message: "You're just my cup of tea."

- A huge orange tied with a red ribbon. Message: "Knock, knock . . . " "Who's there?" "Orange . . . " "Orange who?" "Orange you ever going to be my Valentine?" *OR* "Orange you ever going to . . . (whatever's appropriate)."

Puzzle Your Valentine

1. You'll need a large sheet of white poster board and six red or pink envelopes. As an alternative, simply use regular paper and decorate white envelopes with stripes, dots, etc. You'll also need scratch paper and pencil.

2. On scratch paper, write some simple four-line rhyming Valentine verses. If you use the basic format of that old familiar one,

> "Roses are red
> Violets are blue
> Sugar is sweet
> And so are you,"

you can point out to kids that only the second and fourth lines have to rhyme to make a little verse. Here are some rhyming combinations you might suggest:

- care, share, bear, dare, where, there, hair, rare

- be, see, free, key, me, we, plea, agree, harmony

- June, moon, noon, soon, baboon, cartoon

So, for example, you might use "care" and "there" to create the following:

> "I like you lots
> I really care
> I'll follow you here
> I'll follow you there."

If you happen to have a rhyming dictionary or a dictionary with a rhyming glossary, this is a great time to show kids how to use this resource.

3. Write your Valentine verse, illustrated if you like, using bright-colored markers, so that it covers the entire front side of the poster board.

4. With a pencil, draw a jigsaw puzzle design on the poster board (about 12-15 pieces is a good number). Cut into pieces following your pencil lines.

5. Divide the puzzle pieces among the six envelopes. If possible, deliver the envelopes at hourly intervals throughout the day. If staggered delivery is impossible, it's still fun to receive all the puzzle pieces in an attractively wrapped box.

Mother's Day or Father's Day

Two-Way Scrolls

For kids of all ages:

1. Brainstorm on scratch paper a list of reasons why Mom or Dad is terrific.

2. Using a large piece of paper, decorate the margins with markers. Then write in the center: "It is hereby decreed that Mom (or name or Grandma, etc.) is to be honored on this day, Mother's Day (write in the year) for the following reasons: . . . " Then add the list (if writing by hand, writing against the top of a ruler helps to keep lines straight). If using a computer, set the margins so they are fairly wide and decorate after printing.

For parents:

1. Parents brainstorm on scratch paper reasons why it is great to be a parent to your son or daughter.

2. Follow the above directions, substituting the following: "It is hereby decreed that (child's name) is to be honored on this day, Mother's Day (the year). He (or she) makes it great to be a mother for the following reasons: . . . "

3. After the list is completed, roll the paper up and seal with a sticker or a piece of tape. Tie with a ribbon.

Giant Personalized Crossword Puzzle

1. You'll need a large piece of poster board for this (or as an alternative, you can tape together pieces of paper to make one large sheet), markers, pencil, and paper.

2. Brainstorm a list of answers that will be included in the crossword puzzle. Think about names of family members, including pets; places you've visited on vacation and sights you've seen; favorite movies, books, restaurants, foods, etc. For example, two clues might be "Yellowstone Park" and "tacos."

3. Start with scratch paper and use a basic design from a newspaper's crossword puzzle. But don't worry about keeping the design symmetrical.

4. Using a pencil, fit in the answers to the puzzles, interlocking them in at least one place and reworking your design as you go.

5. When the puzzle is finished, copy the design onto the poster board and color in (or X out) all the squares that won't be used. Number the squares that will be used.

6. On a plain sheet of paper, write or type up the clues. For example, 12 across: "Where we all went on vacation two years ago;" 14 down: "One food we always all agree on."

Make a Memory Book

Following are directions for putting together a little memory book that will give parents and kids an opportunity to talk about experiences they've shared.

1. You can create your own photo album using paper cut to 4" x 6" size and stapled together, or start with one of those little books with plastic sleeves. On the first page, insert a slip of paper that reads "Happy Father's Day" or "Happy Mother's Day" from (your name).

2. On each set of facing pages, insert on the left-hand side a snapshot or, if you prefer, a drawing of something you remember.

3. On the right-hand side, slide in a written paragraph. You might want to make a rough draft first and either print neatly or type up the final copy. In the paragraph, you might talk about what you were doing together in the photo or drawing, what you especially remember about that time, how you feel when you see that photo, etc.

Note: An alternative to the above directions: Using digital photos, create the entire project for viewing on the computer.

Fourth Of July

Personal Declaration of Independence

1. Read aloud as much of the beginning of the Declaration of Independence as you think appropriate for your children's ages. Even very young grade-schoolers can comprehend the general idea.

2. Talk about what the document means historically and what it would also mean for an individual; use the concept of "by myself" for younger kids.

3. Ask kids to write their own personal "Declaration of Independence," which starts like this:

   "When, in the course of human events, it becomes necessary for children to live on their own without their parents, the said children should be capable of and willing to execute the following: . . . "

   What should follow is a list of what each child thinks a young person should be able and willing to do in order to live on his or her own.

4. At the same time, parents might write their own list, based on what elements they see as vital to the independence of their children.

5. Discuss these, noting similarities and differences between the kids' lists and those made by the parents.

Note: After the holiday, you might like to store these "declarations" with that red, white, and blue tablecloth and those miniature flags. A few years later, you might pull these out along with the Fourth of July decorations and make comparisons after everyone has repeated the activity.

Sidewalk Story

If your neighbors spend a lot of time outside on the Fourth of July for fireworks or a block party, use the occasion for a block-long neighborhood "story." You'll need lots of chalk.

1. Encourage whole families to get involved. Talk with your own kids about everyone's right to not participate.

2. On a sidewalk square in front of your house or apartment building, write an intriguing first sentence about Independence Day. Here are a couple of possibilities:

    - It was the Fourth of July, but the sun never came up.

    - Nobody saw who put a hundred flags around the fire hydrant.

3. The stories are then continued on each sidewalk block by different members of the neighborhood. Small children can contribute "decorations" or illustrations. You can stay on one side of the street or continue the story across the street and down the block.

4. Remind the last few writers that they'll have the tricky job of winding up the story!

5. Make a splash party of washing down the sidewalks.

Thanksgiving

Little Baskets of Thanks

1. Early in the day, distribute paper clips and colorful slips of paper (about the size of a ruler) to each family member. Everyone should receive the same number of strips as the number of those who will be seated at the dinner table.

2. Explain that each strip is to be used to write a short message of thanks for something done or said during the last year. These might be sincere or humorous, as simple as "Sis, thanks for always letting me know when my clothes are out of style" or "Mom, thanks for encouraging me to stick with my piano lessons." Children as young as three can be encouraged to dictate their messages.

3. Roll up each strip and fasten with a paper clip. Deposit these in small, individual baskets set at each family member's place at the dinner table.

The Thanksgiving Extravaganza

1. While meal preparations are under way (or the day before), encourage kids and grown-ups as well to plan a play about Thanksgiving to be presented after dinner. Provide some Thanksgiving stories from books previously checked out from the library as a basis for the story line. Here are some ideas if the writers want to come up with their own plot but need a jump start:

   - The Missing Turkey Leg

   - The Mysterious Thanksgiving Guest

   - Taco Salad for Thanksgiving?

   - The Thanksgiving Dinner Mix-Up

   - The Magic Cornucopia

   If ideas are still flagging, try suggesting older kids act out the plot for one of the above as if it were being presented as an episode of their favorite sitcom.

2. Suggest typing out a script. This five-page plan usually works: one page for the beginning of the play (should contain a problem), two to three pages for the middle of the play for trying to solve the problem, and one page for the ending. Print copies for each actor.

3. Provide poster board and markers for titles, set designation ("this is supposed to be an office"), etc. Also provide a boxful of costume materials (old clothes and hats) and allow time for rehearsal.

4. A good time for presentation of the play might be between dinner and dessert.

Round-Robin Thanksgiving Messages

1. Start a letter to family members who aren't able to join you at the table. Pass it on sometime during the day, asking everyone to contribute a few lines. Small children can dictate a message, draw a picture, or "sign" by outlining their hands. Or, perhaps you might all enjoy taking turns at the computer and adding messages to one giant e-mail.

2. Include photos of the day when you send the letter—digital ones taken that day and sent with the e-mail would be great!

It's All About Me!

• •

Joel: I know you chose that title just for me.

Peggy: Oh, you're not so selfish . . . anymore . . .

Joel: Gee. Thanks.

Peggy: But I suppose it was my fault that you were so selfish.

Joel: That's a typical "Mom" comment.

Peggy: No, I'm serious. When you were little, I did everything to help you feel like you were the center of the universe. I took time to do the things you wanted to do and celebrated your every achievement.

Joel: But you did more than that. You always had some creative ideas for things for me to do. I recognize many of them in this chapter.

Peggy: My hope was that I could make writing a natural part of your day—so you wouldn't even know that you were doing it. Just like going out and riding your bike or playing on your computer.

Joel: Again, you're selling yourself short. You did more than that. You actually got down on the floor and worked with me. One of the biggest ways you helped me was not by telling me how to do the project, but doing your own work alongside of me. This kind of "modeling" is one of the most effective ways to teach kids.

Peggy: Plus it's fun for parents as well. And I just love looking over all those things we did back then.

The Toddler as Writer

As soon as the first set of connected words tumble out of a toddler's mouth, a parent can proudly proclaim that child to be a writer. Simply take a blank scrapbook or notebook and copy those first precious spoken words into the book, exclaiming, "'The kitty drinks water.' That's what you said. Look—I wrote it down. Those are your words."

Then, while reading storybooks aloud, point to groups of words, locate the name of the author on the front of the book, point it out, and say, "Look, these are Dr. Seuss's words. He wrote them down—just like I wrote down the words you said today."

Continue the book until children can write on their own—or even beyond if they enjoy dictating stories to you.

Official Birthday Writing Sample

Next to the birthday party snapshots in your photo album, you might like to add the "Official Birthday Writing Sample" each year. Or, if you keep digital photos on a CD, just scan the sample and include it on the disk.

For an effective writing sample, try for a paragraph with sentences rather than merely a list (but certainly go for a list if that's all your child wants to do). A paragraph will show not only the state of your child's handwriting, spelling skills, and vocabulary, but also understanding of organization and syntax.

Here are some sample topic sentences for the "Official Birthday Writing Sample," all designed to reveal your children's thoughts and ideas, as well as their writing ability:

- Here's what I think I'm going to like about being five.

- Eight is better than seven for lots of reasons.

- Here's what I did to celebrate my sixth birthday.

- Some things I know and understand today better than a year ago.

- Now that I'm eleven, I have certain plans.

Note: If your child wants you to type up the list, go along with that idea, because in this activity, the purpose is not to collect handwriting samples—you get those from school all the time. The purpose is to explore the ideas in that newly turned five-year-old brain.

The Giant Birthday Book

Here's a variation of the previous birthday idea.

1. On the first birthday after a child has learned to draw, buy three sheets of poster board—two brightly colored, one white. Ask the child to draw his or her picture in the center of the white poster board.

2. Next, draw spokes radiating from the drawing. On each spoke, ask the child to give a reason why he or she is different than last year. For example:

    - I can reach the faucet without standing on a stool.

    - I learned to play two songs on the piano.

    - I don't worry about the dark as much as I used to.

    - I outgrew last summer's swimsuit.

    - I learned to whistle.

3. If there's space (and sufficient interest), your child might enjoy drawing additional spokes radiating from the reasons and adding more details. For example, "I learned to whistle" might be embellished with thoughts about who taught the whistling skill, how hard it was to learn, what songs are fun to whistle, etc.

4. When the drawing with its spokes is complete, poke two holes on the left side at the bottom and top; cut them into dime-sized holes. Do the same with the two pieces of colored poster board; they will make a cover for the book. Tie together with string or yarn. Add a new poster board drawing each year.

Journals, Journals, and More Journals

In addition to the usual "Today I woke up and had breakfast and went to school" entries repeated in most kids' diaries or journals, there are dozens more ways to make journal-keeping an enticing experience. As a parent, your job is to make suggestions and discuss privacy issues. Here are some ideas:

1. For some kids, a sharp-looking journal or notebook, or one of those little diaries with a key, have enormous appeal. For others, keeping journals in a file on the hard drive is the only way to go.

2. And although journals often record one's own daily experiences, there are a myriad of other reasons some people enjoy keeping journals. For example, you might suggest some of the following:

   - recording dreams

   - writing down ideas for possible inventions

   - making notes for a fantasy world

   - keeping track of the weather

   - keeping track of squirrel or bird activity in the yard

   - recording ideas for drawings or paintings

   - recording events seen from the apartment window

   - writing what Bowser would have to say about the day

   - keeping ongoing notes about a hobby, like rock collecting

3. It's against The Rules to ask questions about anyone else's journal. You might say, "Hmm, I haven't written in my journal for two years, but I'm getting back to it." Or you might like to share something you wrote in your own journal if you're looking for a way to open discussion about journaling. So before starting a diary or journal, your child should be certain what the rules in your house are about privacy.

4. For the child who has a shiny new journal but complains there's nothing to write about, here's a two-month supply for one idea a day:

My idea of a boring day	I'd like to invent . . .
My idea of an exciting day	I'd like to try . . .
My idea of a good movie	I'd like to know . . .
My idea of a good music video	I'd like to have . . .
My idea of a good book	I'd like to . . .
My idea of a good TV show	I'd like to accomplish . . .
My idea of a perfect school	I'd like to investigate . . .
My idea of a perfect parent	What I would never want to do
My idea of a perfect weekend	What I hope I always remember
My idea of a perfect vacation	What I should have known
My idea of a good friend	What I think success is
My idea of a good secret hiding place	What bugs me more than anything
My idea of a good pet	What I'd rather do than anything
My idea of a perfect meal	What I'm proud of
What I think about arguing	My idea of good music
What I think about giving in	My biggest fear
What I think about fighting	My most valued possession
What I think about friendship	My best role model
What I think about jealousy	My best advice
What I think about big cities	I am happiest when . . .
What I think about small towns	I am most miserable when . . .
What I think about homework	Next year, I'll . . .
What I think about making money	Two years from now, I'll . . .
What I think about having pets	Ten years from now, I'll . . .
What I think about the world	Twenty-five years from now, I'll . . .
What I think about this weather	When I'm grown up . . .
What I think about my name	What tomorrow will bring . . .
What I think about art	The future I'll never know . . .
Certain colors affect me	Certain smells affect me

Add-Me-Up Autobiography

With a roll of adding machine tape (call an office supply store), ruler, and a pen, you can help your child create a different kind of autobiography. **Note:** You can also cut ordinary paper into strips for this activity.

1. Have your child mark off one foot of adding machine tape for each year in his or her age. (An eight-year-old will have eight feet.)

2. Cut off the tape and, starting with the first mark, number each year.

3. Try to help your child think of some things he or she experienced during each of these years. Ask questions to start the wheels going: "When did you learn to walk? When did you start preschool?" Next, try to help your child remember something that happened during each school year—like a play the class put on for parents, or Field Day, or learning to write cursive.

   Next, suggest adding any big events in the family, like brothers or sisters being born, or a vacation, or moving. Finally, try to think of things that happen every year, like exchanging valentines or going swimming at the lake. Put these down in any year.

4. Make yourself an adding machine autobiography to share with kids.

   Note: You'll probably want to use five-year segments!

Hairography

A look at your child from the top! You'll need paper or crayons the approximate color of your child's hair and skin (and yours as well, if you intend to participate) along with scissors, some glue or paste, a ruler, and a pencil and pen. You can just use crayons if you can't find the right paper colors.

1. Ask kids to brainstorm, making a list of everything they can think of that has ever happened to their hair. For example: having bows Scotch taped to a bald baby head, too-short haircuts, playing with shampoo suds, getting gum tangled up in hair, arguing with parents about hairstyles, cutting his or her own hair, copying a friend's hairstyle, etc.

2. Now ask kids to write little stories about their hair as if the hair were telling it! You might suggest a sample topic sentence like one of these:

   • "I've had a pretty good life up here on top of Angie's head."

   • "Being Terri's hair is not that easy."

   • "As Rashad's hair, I've got some pretty good stories to tell."

3. Have kids check over stories to make sure they've explained everything clearly and that they've included lots of details.

4. Then have kids cut out, from construction paper, a big oval to represent their faces (or lightly color in plain paper). Using a ruler as a guide, the next step is to write the stories onto the faces with marker or pen.

5. To finish the hairography, kids can "make" hair and glue it on. The hair can either look like it does now or like it used to look. They can make curls by pulling paper strips along the side of scissors, make fringe for bangs, add ribbon bows, or make a construction paper comb or pick to stick out of the top.

   If you have the know-how, this is a fun computer experience, printing the words over an enlarged photo with a blank face.

   Note: Some kids might enjoy taking their hairographies to their salon or barbershop and ask to have them displayed.

Pseudonyms, Serious and Silly

Because many kids today are familiar with the idea of creating passwords, giving themselves a pen name to use with their own writing is not perhaps the challenge it once was. But then again, a pseudonym for written work has no limitations, and no flashing red message will pop up informing writers that their name has already been selected.

You might suggest that a pen name reflect something about the writer by asking the question: "Does my pen name sound like me or someone I'd like to be?" Here are some ideas for helping your young writer choose just the right pen name.

1. Rearrange the letters in the writer's name, using just the last name or all of the letters if desired. For example:

   - an anagram for Epstein is N. I. Steep

   - an anagram for Rachel S. is Charles

2. Choose something geographical for a pseudonym by putting together two place names: Venezuela Washington, for example.

3. Pair the first and last names of two characters from favorite books: Ramona Potter.

4. Pair a favorite first name with the name of a day of the week or a month: Scott January.

5. Make up a triple alliterative (tongue twister) name: Marcus Montgomery Mason.

6. Combine an adjective with a noun for a penname that creates a picture: Rocky Rivers.

Personal Profile Sheet

What if you were a character in a book?

Explain to kids that before authors even start their books, they create a profile sheet for each of their characters. That way, the writer has a handy list (or maybe a whole bulletin board full of notes) to consult when they want to know how their characters would react in certain situations.

Here's a list of items your child might want to fill out as if he or she were slated to be a character in a brand-new novel:

- biggest likes
- biggest dislikes
- how friendly
- how shy
- how self-confident
- temperament
- hopes/goals/dreams
- sense of privacy

- sense of humor
- values: what's important
- values: what's right/wrong
- level of politeness
- capacity to love/hate
- frequency of boredom
- frequency of excitement
- frequency of jealousy

Parents might want to privately fill out a couple of these sheets before the activity, sheets that you will not share with your child: one for what you think your child will say about himself or herself, and another one recording your opinion of each item (for example, how shy you consider your child to be).

Also, you might like to fill out a sheet about yourself to share with your child.

I Used To . . . But Now I . . .

Give this list to a child all at one time or just throw out one once in a while.

I used to think _____ but now I _____

I used to be so _____ but now I _____

I used to want to _____ but now I _____

I used to have _____ but now I _____

I used to worry about _____ but now I _____

I used to hope that _____ but now I _____

I used to feel like _____ but now I _____

I used to wonder if _____ but now I _____

Thank-You Notes

And after all these "all about me" ideas, here's a twist: thinking about someone else—the someone who was nice enough to give "me" a gift.

Here are a few ideas to make those painful thank-you notes go more quickly (e-mail thank-yous—although better than nothing at all—just don't really do the job).

1. Very small children can make handprints using a stamp pad or paint-soaked sponge. Wait until the prints are totally dry and print the message on top, reading it aloud to the children as they work. This gives children an opportunity to participate and to begin to understand what thank-you notes are all about.

2. The beginning writer can make use of fill-in-the-blank cards available at stationery stores. Or parents can print out simple computer-generated messages:

    Dear _____,

    Thank you for the _____.

    Love, _____

3. Invest in return address labels preprinted with your child's name and address. This saves one tedious step in the process. Kids also like filling in blank address labels more than just writing addresses directly on the envelope.

4. Teach (or remind) older kids that the simple "five Ws" always work for thank-yous, just as they do for the news:

    Who — Say something about the person who sent the gift, such as "You always think of stuff I like" or "You must be cold up there in Minnesota this winter."

    What — Say what the gift is: the check, the tool kit, the art set.

Where & When — Say something about where and/or when you'll use the gift. "I'm planning to use the gift certificate the next time we go to the mall" or "I'm keeping the snow globe on my dresser where I'll see it all the time."

Why — Say something about why the gift was appropriate, appreciated, needed, etc. "I have always wanted a microscope" or "I really needed a radio alarm clock to help get me going in the morning."

Another idea: Save artwork your child brings home from school for use as thank-you notes. Turn the work over and write a note on the back.

Chapter 3

A Family of Wordsmiths

• •

Peggy: This is fun. We haven't sat down and done a project together in years. It reminds me of the things we used to do when you were a little guy.

Joel: Yeah, but not all parents have that kind of dedication. It's hard work keeping up with the energy and enthusiasm of a kid. Sometimes it's easier to just let them do what they want.

Peggy: And that's the kind of advice you gave the families you saw in therapy?

Joel: Absolutely not. But I did try to help validate the parents' feelings. And gradually, I helped the families find ways that they could start communicating together more effectively. Using shared activities was always a great starting point.

Peggy: Well, we have quite a few ideas in this chapter.

Joel: The really great thing about these activities is that they help family members gain insight into each other's thoughts and feelings. It's often easy for people to go about their daily lives without ever thinking about what the people around them are thinking and feeling.

Communication Tag

"You're it!" takes on a new meaning in this written version of tag, which can last anywhere from less than a minute—to perhaps years. For this activity, instead of "tagging" someone with a shove, you use a written message that requests a written reply. You might want to start out by simply leaving a note on a child's dresser that reads "The park or the library Saturday? Write me back." The idea is to start up some written correspondence on everyday, objective topics, an activity that may lead to some extended, subjective topics later on—subjects for both written correspondence and real conversations as well.

After some success with a few individual notes for a continuing activity, you might start by purchasing one of those spiral-bound notebooks through which you can stick a small pencil so it will always be handy. Make the first message in the notebook something short, something that allows for a simple response. Also, if the notebook is going to be passed around to various family members, try for a subject that interests everyone in the family. For example, "I noticed that they're already filling the pool at the Community Center; I'm anxious to see this year's schedule. Please pass this on."

The novelty of this activity will probably keep it jogging along for a few days or even a week; then interest may begin to lag. Don't be tempted to push it; just pull out the notebook a couple of times a year and let it run its course. In some families, communication tag may lead to deeper discussion, and while in others "whatever" may be the best response you get, it's good to remember that you're opening another avenue for communication. Steering away from anything that remotely smacks of nagging or teaching a lesson increases the likelihood of participation.

Note: If the journal gets "lost," you may want to put out an APB. If it never shows up and the interest is there, start another one.

An ongoing computer version of Communication Tag would simply have a file reserved for ongoing input from family members by ending an entry with "Okay, Dad, you're it."

Two-Way Journals
(also called "Back and Forth" Journals)

This extended version of the previous activity combines Communication Tag with journal writing (discussed in the previous chapter). A journal or notebook designated for just this purpose starts with an entry from one of the participants on the second page, placing the entry (probably the parent's) on the left-hand side. A topic is chosen—perhaps from the list on page 27. The first participant writes a definition, for example, of a truly boring day; the second participant gives his or her version of a truly boring day on the facing page.

The first participant can continue to choose the subject, or the two can change places, handing off the opportunity to choose the topic.

Using a computer, this is a great after-school check-in activity for a parent who can take a few minutes to generate an e-mail to a child who arrives home first.

For example:

> "Hi Kari, hope you had a good day. I finally got that report finished! Here's my idea of a truly boring day. It's raining and nobody's home but me, and I can't find anything to read. What would your most boring day be like?"

The e-mails can be an activity in themselves, or they could be saved in a special file. Some kids might like to print them out and keep them in a notebook to form a journal.

Hypothetical Questions

Here's a quick after-dinner activity. Give everyone a piece of scratch paper and a pencil. Give the following directions: write "what if" on the paper and then complete the question you dictate. You might want to give some examples (either reality- or fantasy-based):

- What if the electricity went off for a week?

- What if washing machines could truly make clothes brand-new again?

This is a good time to introduce the word "ramifications." For example, the result of no electricity could be that food would go bad in the freezer, and even though everything had thawed, you wouldn't be able to eat it fast enough. If washing machines made clothes brand-new, no adults would actually need to buy clothes, and so they might buy fewer clothes, perhaps making the price of clothes go way up.

After the answers have been written, exchange, then read aloud.

Give positive reinforcement to questions while discussing answers.

Note: An in-the-car out loud version of this activity works (especially for younger children), but the written version gives everyone an opportunity to be creative individually rather than reacting to the ideas others propose and avoids "that-was-what-I-was-going-to-say" squabbling.

Wow! That's Some Good Advice

Do you know what kind of counsel your kids might give on tricky issues?

Scan the newspaper for days when an advice column prints a question appropriate for family discussion (or go to an on-line advice column appropriate for young people). Clip (or print out) the column, but keep the columnist's answer out of sight. Give everyone a slip of paper and ask them to write a response starting "Dear _____," detailing the advice they would give the writer.

Collect all the answers and read them aloud, either mixing in the actual answer or giving it last. If appropriate, make a guessing game out of who wrote what answer. This is a great discussion starter.

Age "Poems"

These "poems" are great for insight into what family members see as the limitations as well as the more positive aspects of various ages. They're really nothing more than expanded lists. Age poems start with a line such as "Being twelve means . . ." or "When you're four . . ." Give kids (and parents) an opportunity to choose any age, explaining that you may select your present age, an age you were many years ago, or even one you won't reach for many years. Suggest writers include both the positives and the negatives. Brainstorm ideas together, help all members of the family get their poems typed up, printed out, illustrated if desired*, and display on fridge.

Note: This is not a poem in the rhyming sense; it is unified because each line starts with the same form of a verb.

Here are a couple of examples:

When you're three, you . . .

• pretend you live in a gingerbread house with a gumdrop roof

• get the drumsticks saved for you

• put your socks on all by yourself

• can count: "one, two, eleven, nine"

• make lipstick pictures on Mommy's new purse

• think your blocks are a giant skyscraper

• talk to Mr. Potato Head like he's going to answer back

• tell the babysitter that you're too big for a hug, but that you need to sleep with Teddy Bear

Turning 50 means . . .

- having the self-confidence—but not the muscle tone—to take up roller-blading, mountain biking, and waterskiing

- pretending a garden salad with a side of melba toast is a cheeseburger with fries

- trading kids for cats

- looking out your windows less and inside yourself more

- taking less out of the checking account and putting more in the savings account

- measuring hours against books read

- realizing the whole world is your neighborhood

*Writers might enjoy gluing poems to a larger piece of construction paper and using cut-outs from magazines to make a collage around the edges. Computer users could insert clip art or other images in the margin before printing.

Writer-of-the-Month

A few times a year (the same number as the number of members in your family), you might use the fridge or another obvious spot to highlight the "writer-of-the-month." The idea here is to show how everyone uses writing. For kids, there are always school papers, but if they know they're going to be the featured writer, perhaps they might like to write a special poem or illustrated story for the occasion.

Parents can do the same—perhaps composing a short paragraph about a childhood memory—although simply hanging up copies of a memo written at work, a letter to an insurance company about a problem with a bill, a planning sheet for a birthday party, etc. all get across the message that writing is something done every day by nearly everyone.

"I See, You See"

Great communication can sometimes result when two or more people record their version of an event, a particular scene, or even an argument. You might start by finding an optical illusion or two (look on the Internet). Spend some time looking at these and then explain that sometimes people aren't actually misrepresenting what they saw; they genuinely saw things differently.

Another way to demonstrate this concept is to show how it applies to movies.

Try this experiment: Show a short (perhaps three-minute) preselected clip from a video. Try to find something that shows two points of view being presented. Then ask family members to write down what they saw. Here are a couple of responses to the famous closet scene from *E.T.* when Elliott's little sister first sees the extraterrestrial creature.

One response: "So the little girl opens the closet and screams really loud because she sees E.T."

Another response: "E.T. is totally terrified because this little girl opens the closet and starts screaming."

Discussing the differences in point of view helps explain this concept. You might talk about how this difference in perception often leads to some viewers thinking a movie is terrific while others don't like the same movie at all.

After trying this exercise with objective subjects, you might move on to having kids write out their versions of a squabble.

Family Ad Campaign

Start by talking about what an ad campaign tries to accomplish. Advertisers try to convince consumers that their clients' cereal, athletic shoes, cars, etc. are the best around. List some of the venues open to advertisers: TV, radio, newspaper and magazine ads, bumper stickers, billboards, etc.

Plan an ad campaign promoting your family by starting with some brainstorming. What makes your family a good one? (Or you might like to substitute another adjective for "good," like "typical," "great," "interesting," "amazing," etc.) What qualities make your family one that other people might want to imitate, find out about, or spend time with?

Note: For the more practical members of the family who feel like there needs to be a reason—albeit a pretend one—for a family to have its own ad campaign, you might suggest one of the following scenarios: Perhaps a TV network is going to do a special with a typical American family, and you're trying to convince them that your family would be their best choice, *OR* perhaps a foreign exchange student is trying to find a family with whom to stay for the following year, *OR* perhaps a famous star is researching her role for a movie and needs a family.

A weekend of inclement weather would provide a great time to develop your ad campaign. Start by coming up with a motto, logo, and/or slogan. Then make billboards (using poster board), brochures, bumper stickers, and even TV and/or radio spots if you have the equipment.

Utilizing various computer software programs to help produce materials for your campaign will increase the appeal of this activity for some kids (and parents as well).

Today's Top Ten List

Here's a quick writing activity perfect for the last few minutes before dinnertime or bedtime.

On a table, place a large piece of paper with ten bright-colored dots evenly spaced down the left side.

At the top, print a heading such as one of the following:

• "Reasons why shoes should not be left on the stairs."

• "Ideas for using the leftover turkey."

• "Problems with staying in the shower too long."

After everyone has had a chance to fill in an answer or two, cut the answers apart (into strips), and let everyone have a turn at rearranging them, explaining what order they chose and why they selected the reason they did as their number one on the "best" list.

You might like to write in the first two yourself, setting the tone for both humorous and serious answers. For example, under "Reasons for not leaving things on the stairs," you might put "People might trip over them and hurt themselves" as well as "They might get sold on eBay."

Vacation Journals

The job of recording the events of the day in a vacation journal is an activity that can help the boring parts of a trip (like long car rides or rainy afternoons), build self-esteem, and preserve memories at the same time.

Here are a few ways to make vacation journal-keeping more fun than tedious:

• Take a scrapbook along on the trip, if possible, along with markers, a pencil, small scissors, and a glue stick. If only one child is in charge, suggest making a title page featuring your child's name in fancy letters identifying the "author." If children will be sharing the activity, let each design individual pages and sign each of those.

• Make use of an instant camera, one-hour developing, or snapshots stored on a digital camera so that the writer can base entries on photos instead of simply relying on memory. Suggest describing the photos both objectively using lots of details, or subjectively, giving the writer a chance to give personal reactions to the scene or event photographed.

• Encourage the use of brochures, pamphlets, maps, postcards, etc. for taking-off points in writing entries. Writing comments on the amenities listed on the hotel leaflet, discussing the room by looking at its photo, or commenting on the "Continental breakfast included" is lots easier when you're working from something concrete rather than just a memory.

• Encourage the writer to include comments from other family members.

• Consider writing each entry on a 4" x 6" index card, which can later be placed into the photo album or scrapbook either under or next to a photo or postcard. Using cards is effective because their size makes them less intimidating than writing in an actual journal; starting over is a cinch.

Family Newsletters

Newsletters have taken on a whole new life since the advent of e-mail, and your family might already enjoy writing the kind of newsletter that instantly reaches family members anywhere in the world. Some families have even created their own Web sites—an engrossing family activity—so that anyone interested, logging on anytime, can view the most recent photos and catch up on the latest happenings.

For others, the pleasure of creating something on paper cannot be achieved virtually. The following tips apply to whichever format you prefer:

- Decide first just exactly whom the newsletter will cover—your immediate family, your extended family (on both sides?), people to whom you are related but are not really in contact with?

- Decide how often your newsletter will be published—once a month, once a year (over the holidays), or maybe you would just like to try a one-time shot at the activity.

- Make interviews an integral part of the newsletter. First-person columns are great ("Last week I broke the school record for free throws in a single season"), but in order to turn the job of communicating the family news into a communication-building activity, talk to each other and include other family members' ideas, opinions, etc.

- Try to keep any one family member from becoming the "headliner" of the issue. Come up with ideas for family members who might not currently be basketball stars. Suggest someone review a new restaurant or movie the family enjoyed together (see chapter 2), or perhaps someone would like to write a description of what he or she sees looking out a bedroom window, along with some personal reflections. Perhaps: "Whenever I see a green car pull up across the street, I know that Todd and Angela's grandparents have driven across the state for the weekend, and I wish my grandparents were here, too."

- Let kids decide if they want to be edited for errors. If your child is seven and misspelling words and writing run-on sentences . . . so what? Spell check will help out some on a computer, but what about leaving the writing alone, allowing children to show off current skill levels (unless you think the handwriting is too difficult to be read at all).

- Remember that newsletters of more than one typed page are more than most people want to read (with the possible exception of grandparents).

- Humor always works—unless it's at someone else's expense. Don't be afraid to show your family's lighter side and to poke gentle fun at yourselves.

The Multi-Caption Photo Adventure

Before new snapshots go into the photo album, try this exercise in better understanding how people look at things from different viewpoints.

Let's say there is a picture that was taken at a backyard barbeque where everyone is seated at the picnic table. Looking at the photo, ask everyone to write a short sentence or two about what they remember about that moment. You might be surprised—or not—to know that your daughter only comments about how she felt miserable all afternoon because she hated the outfit she was wearing, while you might remember that you thought it was terrific that you were still friends with the Wilsons after all these years.

So your daughter writes "Ugh. Worst outfit I ever owned," and you write "We've been friends with the Wilsons for 23 years now." You can slide these in behind the photo, learning more about each other today, preserving personalized memories for tomorrow.

Family Trivia Board Game

Using an old game you no longer play, glue new squares made from heavy paper to the board. These squares should reflect your family in some unique ways. For example, playing the new game you've created, you might land on a square that reads, "Take an extra turn. For the first time ever, everybody made it through our vacation without poison ivy" or "Go back three spaces—whole family spent an hour looking for Puffy."

You might like to start from scratch and make a trivia-based board game in which players move markers around the board by correctly answering questions about family matters.

Examples:

- Names of distant relatives
- Number of states the family has visited
- Dates when family members were born
- Size of the largest room of the house or apartment
- First car family owned

Start by drawing out the game board on poster board; create rules for the game together. Then let everyone write out trivia cards with the questions on the front and the answers on the back. Disagreements about the correct answer can lead to some interesting discussion and fact-checking. For larger families, playing on teams makes the game go more quickly and can even the playing field.

Family History

People have made writing a family history into a lifetime endeavor. But here's a short-term, engaging family history project that provides some insight into the family's background.

Using sheets of paper to represent decades, lay out enough sheets on the floor to represent the number of decades it takes to go back to your child's great-grandparents' births. For most kids today, that would involve around ten sheets of paper. Then with a bright marker, label each of those at the bottom and top.

For example, the most current sheet would be labeled with "2000" at the bottom and "2010" at the top. The sheet on which your child's great-grandparents were born might be labeled "1910" at the bottom and "1920" at the top.

Starting with the most current sheet, draw a line that represents the current year, label it, and write "You are here." Then, moving backwards, have family members draw lines indicating their birth years and label. Just for fun, you might want to wait for visiting grandparents, aunts, uncles, and cousins to label their own lines during their visits.

Next, mark other important events in your family's history, such as deaths, marriages, graduations, moves, major trips, etc. You might even assign a different color marker for each type of event.

After you've spent some time marking, measure distances. For example, you might compare the distance between the time you were born and the time your first child was born; then compare that to the measurement between the time your parents were born and the time the oldest of your siblings was born.

Tape the sheets together and fold accordion-style for storage.

Chapter 4

Take a Bite . . .
Stop and Write

● ●

Joel: Ah! Food. Our family's specialty.

Peggy: Are you being sarcastic again?

Joel: No. I'm serious. Some of my fondest family memories involve food.

Peggy: Really? You've never shared that with me.

Joel: It's true. I love coming home to a steaming bowl of Dad's soup. I remember all those picnics where you packed enough to feed a small nation. And I'll never forget how Grandma used to make two kinds of deviled eggs and cut them either horizontally or vertically to indicate which was which.

Peggy: I can't believe you remember *that.*

Joel: I guess that's our point here. Eating is such a central part of so many families' lives, and food can be associated with so many memories.

Peggy: Like when we had to make you sit at the dinner table for hours until you ate your brussels sprouts?

Joel: You had to bring that up? But yeah, not all food memories are pleasant. To this day I won't eat Jell-O. You only served that to me when I was sick.

Peggy: But I thought it would help you feel better.

Joel: It probably did. But now I have that association. And that's what's so cool about food. Everyone reacts to the same foods in different ways. And often people feel quite passionate about the foods they like—and dislike.

Peggy: That's why writing about food can be so much fun.

Munching Memories

Here's a great way to capture all those food-related family memories.

1. Decide on approximately ten holidays or special occasions your family celebrates. Divide a notebook or scrapbook into the same number of sections. On the first page of each section, neatly print the name of the holiday or celebration.

2. Starting with the first section in your book, ask family members to think of memories they have about foods served for this occasion. Listen carefully to what they say, and then write down what they said in your own words. Here are some examples:

   We always have brownie a la mode on the Fourth of July. First there is the big gooey brownie. Then there is a large scoop of frosty vanilla ice cream. On top of that is a nice warm topping of chocolate sauce. Then we stick a little flag into the sauce. Everybody gets one. (Melissa, age 8)

   At Thanksgiving, everybody likes sweet potato pie. My cousins and I always used to have a contest. As soon as those pies came out of the oven, we'd start cutting them up and betting who could eat the most slices. And it doesn't seem like anybody ever ended up with a stomachache. (Grandpa)

3. Put one memory on each page. It would be nice to have about three to four memories for each section. Add illustrations, cut from magazines or drawn, if you like. If your family has extra snapshots, you could include them in the book.

4. Save the finished scrapbook for a special family occasion. Then pass it around the dinner table during dessert and watch all the smiles.

Alternately: Make a computer version of this project. Ask family members to e-mail responses to your questions. Put the finished product together with digital photos, clip art, etc., and e-mail it to family members.

Food Fight

Families will probably never stop arguing about what's for dinner. But here's a fun way to fight about what should be on the menu.

1. Ask everyone to pretend for the moment that only eight items from the grocery store will be found in the kitchen cabinet and/or refrigerator for the following two weeks. No eating out at restaurants is allowed; no meals at Grandma's. For two weeks, everyone must eat only those eight particular items.

2. Give all participants a sheet of paper and ask them to privately* prepare a list of what they think those eight items should be.

3. At the signal, everyone displays the lists. Place items everyone has in common on a master list.

4. The food fight begins. Discussion starts as all participants defend items on their lists; to begin, you might ask everyone to cross out the least desirable item. Disagreement may ensue as discussions tackle issues of health, taste, and boredom, etc.

5. When activity begins to bog down, explain the one remaining rule: only foods agreed on by all participants will be included. In other words, if only milk and fig cookies are endorsed by everyone, that's exactly what will be eaten for a week. At this point, allow time for individual lists to be amended.

6. The activity ends when everyone comes to a consensus on eight items—or when it looks like a mediator would have to be called in.

*Younger children might need to dictate their lists.

Neighborhood Recipe Book

1. Start by asking neighbors if they would like to contribute a favorite recipe to a neighborhood cookbook. Explain that you're going to include a little information with each recipe; ask the following questions:

- Names of all family members

- Ages of children

- Pets (type and name)

- How long the family has lived in the neighborhood

- Why family members like the recipes or some comments on when and how the recipes have been served

- Family phone number and/or e-mail (optional)

Note: You might want to think up some of your own questions, too.

2. Put that information into a paragraph. For example:

Mr. and Mrs. Brown (John and Ruth) have three children: Teresa 9, George 7, and Tammy 3. They also have a cocker spaniel named Mutt. The Browns have lived in the neighborhood for seven years. Mrs. Brown says this recipe for chili is easy to make and tastes great in cold weather. George contributed his recipe for banana splits, and Tammy dictated her recipe for making pudding in a shaker. Mr. Brown is famous in the neighborhood for his cheesecakes.

Even small children can be encouraged to include recipes: either one typed up for them by a parent or, for example, their handwritten directions for making macaroni and cheese from a box.

3. Come up with a recipe form for neighbors to follow. For example:

- On the top line, please type what kind of recipe you are contributing (main dish, appetizer, dessert, etc.)

- Under that, type the title of the recipe

- Under that, type your name

- Under that, type ingredients needed

- Under that, type the directions

4. Make a title page and a cover for your recipe book using drawings or computer designs. Also make divider pages for each type of recipe that will be included in your book—as well as a page that says "Neighbors" for the section that will include all the neighbor paragraphs you put together.

5. Sort all of your recipes and organize the book.

6. You might want to take a few minutes to go back to your neighbors and have them check over the recipes and paragraphs for accuracy. Allow them a little time to make corrections if necessary. You might want to consider using e-mail for some of the neighbor contacts.

7. Make enough copies for each family in the neighborhood. You might like to host a potluck get-together where every family brings one of their dishes, and you distribute copies of the cookbook.

Raving Restaurant Reviews

If your family eats out often, turn yourselves into reviewers. Next time you have the opportunity to eat at a restaurant, you can become a food critic. This exercise promotes keen observation.

1. Take paper and pen with you; take some notes about the following:

   - How the restaurant looks (style, colors, decorations, etc.)

   - How long it takes to get your food

   - How friendly servers are

   - How many different items are available

   - Anything special they have for kids

   - What days and hours they are open

2. You might want to find other kids and their parents who've eaten at this restaurant and ask their opinion. Try to get specific information. For example:

   - "The fries are always real crispy." Janie, age 7

   - "Kids' meals are too little." Marcus, age 9

   - "I love the Strawberry Swirl Sundae." Tammy, age 6

3. Have your family write a review together. Put the information from the notes you took at the restaurant in the first paragraph and the quotes from the kids in the second paragraph. Here's a sample:

   Capper's Restaurant is a great place to go for families. It's bright and cheerful with big turquoise-and-orange diamonds decorating the walls and booths. They bring the food very quickly, and the waitresses are funny. Don't go here, though, if you want a lot of choices from a kids' menu. Mainly they just have hamburgers. The kids' specials come with a coloring book and a box of four crayons.

Jaimie Allen, age 9, who goes to Capper's about once a week, has a favorite burger. "I just love the Mexican Burger," he says, "because it's just covered all over with guacamole." Tina Starforth, age 11, says, "Try their cherry colas." Tina's mom, Nancy Starforth, says she can always count on Capper's tuna melt.

You might like to deliver or mail your review to the owner of the restaurant. Save an extra copy of each of your reviews, and when you have six or more, staple them together and send them (or e-mail them) to the food editor of your local newspaper.

Become a Family of Consumer Watchdogs

A watchdog guards valuable property; a consumer watchdog makes sure products are worth buying. This exercise promotes assertiveness by learning to communicate wants and needs.

1. Think of something you eat every day: cereal, for example. When you watch the TV ads for this cereal, look for promises the ad makes. Ask yourself if this cereal tastes as good as others of the same kind. Think about what you would do to improve the cereal or what you would do to get more people to buy it. When you have some ideas, write a letter to the company that makes the cereal. Here are some examples:

   - Your ad says, "more raisins in every spoon." I'd like to know—more raisins than what? What are you comparing it to? I really don't think it has all that many raisins. In fact, I think you should put more in.

   - I really like your cereal, but my mom complains that it's not very nutritious. If you'd add some extra vitamins, my mom would let me eat it more often.

2. Get the company address by:

   a) Looking for the address on the product, or

   b) Dialing 1-800-555-1212 to see if the company has a toll-free number (there's no charge to dial an 800 number) and then ask for the address, or

   c) Looking on the product itself for an e-mail address or searching for an on-line Web site, or

   d) Asking grocers if they can get you the address

3. Send your letter by regular mail or e-mail.

Note: Kids should always get permission from parents before sending letters to someone they do not personally know. However, if it's okay with parents, be sure to include a way for the company to respond to the letter—either via return address or e-mail. Companies receive hundreds of letters each year, so they usually don't respond personally. However, it is not uncommon for them to send a generic response or even some coupons.

How to Make a PBJ

1. Give everyone a sheet of paper and a pencil (or access to a computer). Then, have them write clear and simple directions for making a peanut butter and jelly sandwich. Place everyone's completed instructions facedown in a pile on the kitchen table.

2. Place a jar of peanut butter, a jar of jelly, a loaf of bread, and a knife next to the pile of instructions. Ask everyone to gather around.

3. The first volunteer takes the top sheet, turns it over, and slowly reads the first set of directions exactly as written. Someone else volunteers to make a sandwich following those directions. This is a great activity to demonstrate the value of writing precisely!

Examples:

"Put the peanut butter on the bread and the jelly on top of that."

(Sandwich maker puts the jar of peanut butter on the loaf of bread and tries to put the jar of jelly on top of that.)

"Take some bread out of the bag and spread peanut butter on the bread."

(Sandwich maker removes five or six slices and starts to spread peanut butter on all of them.)

"Put the jelly slice on top of the peanut butter slice."

(Sandwich maker puts jelly slice faceup on peanut butter slice.)

The Great, Never-Ending Chili Experiment

Here's an opportunity to open up a discussion by using the metaphor of an evolving recipe. The idea here is that families are always changing, refining, retrieving earlier ideas, rules, values, etc.

1. Choose a dish your family loves, such as chili—something that keeps evolving because you change it slightly almost every time you make it. The larger the number of ingredients in the recipe, the better the experiment. Other ideas, besides chili, include such items as homemade pizza, hot fudge sauce, French toast, macaroni and cheese, etc.

2. Write out the recipe in its present incarnation, date it, and save it (or type it and place it in a newly created directory on the computer).

3. Print the recipe out, and the next time you're ready to make a pot of chili, use a red pen to make corrections, additions, comments about what you changed, how it turned out, etc.

4. Put the recipe in a safe place, ready for the next time you prepare the meal. Or back at the computer, copy and paste the original recipe and correct it so it reflects the changes you made. Add the date and save.

Note: Always remember to save each version. After a few years (or even months), you'll likely be surprised at what you'll find looking back through the various versions. Reading through these versions can be a great conversation starter. Older kids can often grasp the idea of how this activity mirrors the way in which people approach any number of activities in their lives. While looking at the changes in the recipe, the conversation can easily be steered to other areas—such as how family members' thoughts, feelings, and behaviors have changed over the years.

Guess What I Just Ate!

This activity provides instant insight into each family member's sense of adventure as well as practice in descriptive writing!

1. Put a small food item into each of five or six opaque-covered containers. These items should be readily distinguishable for their texture, taste, smell, or perhaps even the sound they make when bitten. Ideas: hot pepper sauce, marshmallows, orange halves, banana slices, caramels, potato chips, etc.

2. Leave these containers in the kitchen and gather the family in another room.

3. The first participant goes into the kitchen, opens a container, eats the item (or just looks at it), and writes a description. HOWEVER, the description should say nothing about what the item looks like (i.e., size, shape, colors, etc.). The clues should use other sensory descriptions (i.e., the taste, smell, or texture of the food). Additionally, encourage participants to use only sensory description and not statements of who likes the food, where it can be bought, how it is grown, etc.

4. Everyone should get a chance to describe at least one item. Afterwards, have everyone read their descriptions aloud and have others guess what item they described.

Eat Your Words!
(An activity for beginning writers)

Here's an entertaining way for parents to spend some time with an early writer and reinforce skills in the process.

1. Buy two packages of pretzels: pretzel sticks and pretzel circles (you might be able to find these combined in one package).

2. For the tiniest child (one old enough to eat pretzels, that is), show a large printed letter and have the child reproduce that letter using the pretzel sticks and circles. Encourage the child to gobble up the letter once s/he has successfully (or with your help) reproduced it with pretzels. Gleefully announce, "You're munching that 'T.' Don't 'Ts' taste delicious?"

3. A slightly older child will enjoy reproducing a word or two. Even a first-grader will enjoy making and munching the tough words from the week's spelling list.

Menu Mania (version one)

In this activity, kids get an opportunity to select a meal of their choice, write out the menu, the shopping list, and the plan for preparation. Of course, parents will need to assist younger children. But as they get older, kids should be able to get the hang of planning and carrying out a meal totally on their own, particularly when written planning is encouraged. This is an excellent exercise for parents to use to promote planning and responsibility. It also provides them a perfect opportunity to reinforce mature behavior.

1. Plan a meal (making sure the ingredients are within the family budget). Looking through cookbooks or even Internet sources will lead to new ideas.

2. Write out the menu as it might appear at a restaurant. (A decorated copy might be centered on the dinner table.)

3. Make a list of necessary ingredients.

4. Check the cupboards, freezer, and fridge for what items will have to be bought. Make a list.

5. Make a written plan for when each step of the meal will be done.

   For example:

4:15	Mix up brownies and put in oven to bake.
4:30	Set the table.
4:40	Make the salad.
4:45	Check brownies and remove from oven when done.
5:00	Boil spaghetti.
5:05	Warm bottled sauce.

6. Be sure cook receives a couple of "Hurrahs!"

Menu Mania (version two)

1. Give each member of the family a pencil and three sheets of paper labeled breakfast, lunch, and dinner. (Small children can dictate their ideas.)

2. Ask everyone to write down the perfect, ideal, nothing-could-be-better menu for each meal. Cost is irrelevant; you're millionaires while you're participating in this activity.

3. Post on refrigerator or bulletin board and wait for "yums" and "yucks" and a spirited discussion.

Chapter 5

Pages and Pages of . . . Sports Pages

• •

Joel: Umm . . . I think you're going to have to handle this one. It's way outside my area of expertise.

Peggy: You mean because you were always told to bunt whenever you got up to bat in Little League?

Joel: Yeah. That's for starts.

Peggy: And you broke your arm on the rings in gym class?

Joel: Okay. That, too.

Peggy: And you quit the wrestling team after two weeks of practice?

Joel: Ouch! I think you've got the idea.

Peggy: But don't you always watch KU's basketball team as they make their way to the Final Four?

Joel: Sure.

Peggy: And haven't you been to your share of Cardinals' games?

Joel: Yeah.

Peggy: Then these exercises won't be so foreign to you.

Joel: I'm just saying that I'd rather read a good book than get out on the court.

Peggy: But you have to admit that sports are full of stories. And where there are stories, there are things to write.

Joel: That's true. And there's always the aspect of discipline, sportsmanship, and teamwork. Those are important things to learn from athletics.

Peggy: But it's much more than that. For each match, for every game, you've got a whole story: the background, the struggle, the characters, and how they function as winners and losers. You've got a variety of points of view—the opinions of every armchair coach.

Joel: I didn't realize you were such a sports enthusiast.

Peggy: I'm not really. I just recognize a good opportunity when I see one. Plus, you never know. Maybe one of the following activities will lead to a new family interest in basketball, baseball, or bowling.

"Fan"tastic Fan Mail

Hundreds of professional sports organizations support Web sites where fans can send e-messages to individual players; millions of fans take advantage of that opportunity. So go ahead and use a search engine to locate your favorite team and to communicate your thoughts. But, the truth is, nothing can take the place of an old-fashioned snail-mail fan letter, especially one written with a marker in a seven-year-old's best printing. Take advantage of those Web sites, however, to find teams' postal addresses (or ask your local librarian for help).

Note: Begin this activity by discussing with your child what the limitations are in your house about sending out mail (e-mail or regular) that includes personal information.

1. Before starting, spend a little time on some of these prewriting activities; that way you'll have some specifics for the contents of the letter.

    -   Research stats, either on-line or using library sources.

    -   Brainstorm a list of what is admirable about the recipient of the letter (here's a good opportunity to talk about sportsmanship, the idea of a team player, modesty, contributions to the community, role models, etc.).

    -   Re-watch videos of particular games.

    -   Read a biography about the athlete.

2. Using standard letter form (even if it's on a computer template) will reinforce this highly useful skill. Some kids may enjoy creating their own letterhead on the computer, one they can file and use later for fan mail and other correspondence.

3. You might suggest this method for composing the letter:

    -   Start with a sentence saying who you are and why you are writing ("I'm in sixth grade, and I'm your biggest fan").

- In the first paragraph, include some of the information from your prewriting activities. For example: "I can't believe you didn't start playing basketball until you were fifteen," or "That final play in the Oklahoma/Nebraska game was the coolest thing I've ever seen."

- In the second paragraph, you might wish the player good luck or even ask for a photo or autograph (although the chances for an answer to that request diminish in direct proportion to the player's popularity). The likelihood of personal responses increases when something "extra" is included: a photo of the fan in a basketball uniform, for example, or a newspaper article about the athlete clipped from a local newspaper.

4. Whether the letter has been written in pen or typed, a hand-printed envelope will get more notice. A younger child might need to practice first on a rectangle drawn the size of the envelope.

Around The Diamond

Here's a little activity to kick off the baseball season. Start by thinking of a sport that contrasts well with baseball. This activity works well when parent and child brainstorm ideas together to come up with one finished product. Examine the following example together—it's about two board games rather than two sports, so as not to spoil your originality.

Scrabble*

Quiet, Brainy

Rearranging, Thinking, Concentrating

Tiles, Racks—Hotels, Deeds

Buying, Trading, Arguing

Noisy, Greedy

Monopoly**

* "Baseball" will go here.

** The name of some other sport will go here.

You'll need lined paper and a pencil. Here are the directions:

1. On line one, write the word "baseball." (You'll be writing your poem on seven lines.)

2. On line seven, write the name of a sport you consider to be very different from baseball.

3. On line two, write two adjectives, words that, to you, describe the sport. Make sure your top line is centered under your first line. Put commas between your words.

4. On line six, write two adjectives that describe the sport you've chosen for line seven. Put commas between your words.

5. On line three, write three action words ending in "ing" (participles) that describe baseball. This line should be longer, with the first two lines centered above it. Put commas between your words.

6. On line five, write three participles that describe the sport on line seven.

7. On line four, write two nouns describing baseball. Then make a dash and write two nouns describing the other sport. Put commas between the first two words and the last two words.

Your baseball diamond is now complete.

Copy it onto unlined paper using a ruler and draw a diamond around it and display.

The Ultimate, Incredible Dream Play

1. Choose a sport in which incredible plays sometimes happen. This activity works for any such sport, but you might want to try football, soccer, or basketball.

2. Decide whether you want to use a real team and actual players or make up a team and players from your imagination. If you do, you can make yourself the quarterback, the goalie, or the forward!

3. Pretend you are the sportscaster describing to a radio audience the most incredible play he or she has ever seen. Since there's no way for that audience to see what actually is happening—or even an instant replay—everything will have to be described in complete detail.

4. After family members have written out their dream plays, they might have some fun reading them aloud to each other, just as if they were breathless sportscasters.

Note: You might want to decide ahead of time if the dream plays must be physically possible or whether fantasy can be involved!

Play-by-Play by You

Here's another opportunity to play sportscaster/sports reporter. It also provides a chance to talk about subjectivity and how differently certain events can appear in the eyes of two eyewitnesses. Practice with this activity may help everyone understand the importance of taking a moment to try and understand each other's point of view.

1. While watching a game on TV, be ready to record five minutes of play from a professional or college game (volleyball, soccer, football, basketball, etc.).

2. Later, watch the play together. Turn down the sound and pretend you're a sportscaster by seeing how well you can each give the play-by-play.

3. Next, write up the play and then compare it to the version that appears in the local papers the next day.

Invent-a-Sport

Here's an activity that will give you the opportunity to create a brand-new sport, perfectly suited for your family, whether your family consists of one four-year-old and one parent, or two parents, six kids, and a couple of grandparents! This is a great cooperative venture, and it really hits home the importance of rethinking and revising.

1. Drag out all the sports equipment you can find around the house: baseballs, tennis rackets, soccer balls, etc. Then add a few extra items like leftover lumber, bricks, buckets, etc. Add some timers, large sheets of paper, and markers for scorekeeping and writing out rules.

2. Working together, make up a new sport involving whatever pieces of sports equipment you wish. Title the game and write out a complete set of rules. Number the rules so that you can refer to one rule or another. Be as detailed as possible; try to cover every scenario.

3. Try out one game/match/round. At this point, it will most probably become necessary to make adjustments. Note that as you go back to "fix" certain rules, it will often become necessary to adjust others as well. Rewriting on the computer will be far less tedious; however, rather than just revising what's on the screen, copy each attempt, save as different versions, and then paste and make the changes. That way you can go back to version one and trace the evolution of your rules. Explain to everyone that "getting there" is half the fun of this exercise. First attempts will usually not work out well, and the idea is to learn from those early false starts.

Your family might enjoy giving a party for other families with your new "sport" as the featured entertainment. Kids will enjoy making up invitations that proclaim the invention of your sport. Copies of the rules can be included with the invitations to give guests a heads-up.

Super Sports Journals

Here's a way to take a shared interest in one particular sport or team and turn it into a family-focused writing activity.

1. A few weeks before the season begins, set up a journal for your family's favorite team or for your child's team. You might want to buy a loose-leaf notebook or set up a special folder on the computer.

2. Start with a special file (or notebook section) labeled "Prediction." Each family member would enter their outlook for the season here, along with special advice they would give to the players or coach.

3. As the season progresses, take turns recording stats, adding comments or highlights, listing player information, etc. Family members can write their take on game days (i.e., what went wrong, what could have gone better, comments on outstanding plays and players, etc.). For professional or college teams, you might paste in (or scan) articles from newspapers and magazines. For kids' teams* you might take photographs at games and include those along with identification information and comments.

*This is an especially good activity for brothers and sisters of team members. It gives them an extra reason (and incentive) for attending their siblings' games.

What a Good Sport!

Turn a ride in the car into an outline for an essay (the best kind—one that doesn't actually ever have to be written!).

1. Brainstorm together a list of qualities that make for good sportsmanship. Ask if anyone can think of any examples of being a good sport, ones they've personally witnessed either from watching a game or playing on a team.

2. Orally organize the main points of your essay. Let's say you'd be limited to only three qualities of good sportsmanship; decide which ones you would choose and in what order you would discuss them—prioritize in order to "save the best for last."

Note: Other sports topics to organize for imaginary essays include "What makes a good team player?" and "What makes a good coach?"

Astounding Stories of Super Sports Heroes

This is a use-your-imagination, back and forth activity—and another good entry in the passing-time-in-the-car category. One person starts, and then the story is passed back and forth orally, with each participant using information about the sport to add to the saga. It never needs to be written—it's the brain work that makes this a great prewriting activity in itself.

1. Choose a sport, a decade, and a "legendary" player—along with an adjective to describe her or him. Then add the words "but the problem was." For example: "In the eighties, there was an incredible tennis player by the name of Nini Niniwitz, but the problem was . . ." *OR* "In the thirties, no one was a more powerful baseball player, no one a better hitter than Mad Murray McMurray, but the problem was . . ."

2. Then go on to describe the exploits of your hero in detail. Come up with incredible athletic feats but make sure that one problem is solved only to have another one crop up—a cliffhanger. This is a great activity to keep ongoing over a period of weeks, picking up where you left off.

Note: A spin on this activity is the sci-fi sports hero route—where stupendous sports feats, unheard of in our time, take place in the future.

Prepositional Plays

Pick a sport, any sport, and give everyone a copy of the following list of words (specifically, prepositions):

above	during
according to	from
against	in back of
around	in front of
at	in spite of
because of	inside of
before	near
behind	on
below	on top of
beside	outside
between	thanks to
by	under
despite	with
down	without

Ask participants to write a "poem" (really just a list of phrases) using as many of the above as possible at the beginning of each line. The last line may begin with a noun or pronoun (she, the quarterback, the goalie, the diver, the speed skater, etc.).

The following poem is about a word game rather than a sport so as not to spoil the originality of any of the participants in your particular choice of game, but it gives the general idea:

According to the rules,
Against all probabilities,
Between the words "snow" and "today,"
Despite the lack of any vowels,
Without using the dictionary,
Thanks to my English teacher,
On top of a triple-word square,
In spite of my sister's nagging to hurry up,
I made 67 points.

Become Experts on a Little-Known Sport

Curling, lacrosse, bocce ball, water polo, dodgeball, kayaking, and at least a hundred other sports out there, ones that few people witness and fewer people actually ever play, are just waiting to be investigated by curious families.

After brainstorming all the possibilities by searching for little-known sports on the Internet, decide together on one that intrigues everyone.

Rather than the writing itself, this activity emphasizes the writing skill of organization. Make a scrapbook, either on paper or computer, and divide it into categories such as the following: history of the sport, rules, object of the game, size of teams, famous players, famous games or matches, regions where sport is played, stories, books, or movies that include references to the sport, etc. Then simply cut and paste, or photocopy and paste, and put together everything you need to become experts.

Chapter 6

Just for Fun . . . Designing Your Own Activities

• •

Joel: This is the perfect time for a line I used to love to say when I was conducting family therapy sessions.

Peggy: What's that?

Joel: "I don't know what I'm talking about."

Peggy: You actually said that to families you saw?

Joel: On more than one occasion.

Peggy: I'm sure that inspired confidence . . .

Joel: Once they understood what I meant, it did.

Peggy: And what did you mean?

Joel: That I could give them plenty of advice and pointers, but it was ultimately up to them to decide how to best live their lives.

Peggy: Even if that meant continuing to hurt each other?

Joel: Once they learned how to really communicate with one another, it never came down to that.

Peggy: So that was your real goal—helping families communicate?

Joel: Absolutely.

Peggy: Umm . . . sorry, but I think we're off on a tangent here. Exactly what does this have to do with the current chapter?

Joel: Everything. This is the point where we get to say, "We don't know what we're talking about."

Peggy: Gee. Thanks.

Joel: No, really. This book is filled with some excellent ideas for families to try out, and I think when they do they'll really learn a lot about themselves. And that's a great thing. But we don't really know how to make these exercises work for the families who will be reading our book.

Peggy: Oh! Now I get it. And the exercises in this chapter are all designed for families to modify to meet their needs. We give them the foundation, and they build the rest.

Joel: Exactly. And in the process, they'll learn more about solving conflict, communicating, and compromise.

Peggy: All of which are important. But don't forget the equally important areas of reaching out to others and celebrating with each other.

Compromise Island

Here's an idea for taking a look at the idea of compromise. The activity mostly involves talking but starts from each player's written list. This particular version revolves around an imaginary island, but you could use any premise as a taking-off point. Here's an example of how it works.

The premise: What if you inherited an unoccupied tropical island along with lots and lots of money—on the condition that all of the money be used for improvements or enhancements to the island? This island features perfect weather, shark-free waters, a small inland lake, hills easy enough to climb, lots of small animals (but none that are dangerous), lots of trees and tropical fruits and flowers—but also enough cleared flat land to make building possible.

Oh, and transportation to and from the island will already have been arranged for—no need to spend any money on that. What would your own priorities for this island be? How would those priorities compare with others in your family?

You'll want to prepare the following before you begin (again, adjust preparations to the scenario you and your family have invented):

1. On a large sheet of poster board, draw an irregularly-shaped island. Indicate a lake, hills, a forest, and/or jungle areas, etc. by designating them with marker.

2. Place 75 (this is an arbitrary number) toothpicks (or other small matching items) in sandwich bags, one bag for each participant. Also, give everyone a pencil and paper.

3. Begin the activity by asking everyone to privately make a list of ten top priorities. Explain that each person should write down what he or she thinks should be added to the island (money is no issue). The items on the list must be concrete in the sense that they must have a fixed material value. For example, while "friendliness" and "peace" are fine ideas, they are also abstract. (Refer to chapter 7, section on nouns, if

necessary.) The writing of this list is the crux of the activity. However, it's also only a starting point because no one is required to stick to the original list. Observing how readily family members change their priorities or steadfastly hang on to them can be an incredibly telling activity.

4. Give all participants an opportunity to mark (in pencil) the spot on the poster board island where they would like to locate their number one priorities.

5. Now the compromises begin. For example, if two players decide on a luxury hotel where friends can stay when they come to visit, a compromise should be made about, for example, where the hotel should be located.

    Compromises can simply be agreed on verbally or decisions can be "bought"—that is, one participant can agree to give another participant "X" number of toothpicks for the right to make a decision.

    The compromise process works best when players realize what other items will be at stake so that they have wagering leverage. For example, perhaps Participant A will give up the decision about where the hotel should be located, trading that decision for the right to name the hotel with no payment.

    Eventually, the need for many decisions will pop up, including perhaps the following:

    -   The right to name lakes, parks, buildings, etc., with the top prize, perhaps, being the right to name the island itself.

    -   The laws—rules and regulations—for running the island.

    -   The level of development. Will the island remain basically primitive, or will it be a model for cutting-edge technology?

    -   The leadership roles on the island.

    -   Ecological and aesthetic issues on the island: Will billboards be allowed, logging; what will happen to refuse, etc.?

At some point, suggestions for the "general good" may come up. For example, someone might suggest that everyone should put in something toward, say, garbage collection, while others may not wish to spend their money in that way.

6. When the first of the participants has spent all of his or her toothpicks, announce that only 15 minutes remain in the game (or other previously designated amount of time). **Note:** The toothpicks will be worthless at that time. In other words, it doesn't do you any good to come out with a bunch of saved-up toothpicks. The first participant continues to be involved as trades and/or compromise situations may arise.

7. When the activity ends, participants examine and discuss:

    a) The state of the island as a whole

    b) Their individual contributions to the island

    c) The role, if any, they have created for themselves on the island

    d) A comparison of each participant's original priority list to one drawn up at the end of the game.

Write Short

From the very long activity above, the focus shifts to one that emphasizes brevity. Here's a challenge: Find out how well your family members can "cut to the chase," an important communication skill.

Strange as it may seem, it's just as challenging to write something in a few words as to write a 50-word paragraph. Everyone will turn into believers when they try shortening some really long sentences so that they (1) still make sense and (2) include all the vital information contained in the first sentence.

You might begin by talking about telegrams, explaining that although they were the fastest method of communication for people at the time they were first used, people did have to pay by the word and, therefore, tried to make their messages as brief as possible. One of the telegraph writers' first realizations in composing their telegrams was how unnecessary articles (the, an, a) really are and how unimportant it becomes to write in complete sentences.

Here's the first challenge. Shorten this long message that Aunt Sally wants to send:

> "I wanted you to know that I am coming to spend some time with you next month on the first day of February, hoping that the train arrives at noon as it is supposed to, and I am planning to stay until the very last day of March, which will be Thursday, the 31st, on which day my train is also supposed to leave precisely at noon."

Challenge A:

Can you shorten that long, drawn-out (67-word) message down to 12 words or fewer? Let everyone try before you look up one possible solution for this word problem. (Solutions are at the end of the chapter.)

Below are a few more challenges for your family to try. These are probably best served up one at a time, after dinner, with a few months in between.

Again, remember to emphasize the paying-for-each-word aspect and to give reminders about unnecessary articles in this activity.

Challenge B:

"Sometime or other during the next year, I am planning to completely cut down the oak tree in the backyard and hope to replace that oak tree with an addition to the yard of some kind of a flowering tree that will be extremely attractive."

Challenge C:

"What you need to do is to walk three blocks in a row all the way from Main Street to Elm Street, moving in a southerly direction."

Challenge D:

"Yesterday I actually won the decathlon and, in addition, not only that, but, for your information, I amazingly broke the county record, one that had not ever been broken for over 20 years, 21 to be exact."

Challenge E:

"This unbelievably delicious recipe for brownies contains, of all things, a carton of yogurt, an ingredient that, in my mind anyway, adds to the moist quality of the finished product."

Extreme Challenge:

This challenge does not involve a set example like the ones above, but rather a conflict or problem taken from daily life. Family conflict is often exacerbated by an individual's tendency to bring in too many irrelevant issues. However, to begin this extreme challenge, family members should be encouraged to first write out their viewpoint of the problem using as many details as possible. Then, using the exercises above as a model, they should try to shorten their description to the fewest and most important details. When taken as an exercise in this manner, problems can often be thought of in a more objective and less personalized manner.

Cut-up Communication

Here's another activity for practicing brevity. Again, note: Rules of grammar and punctuation must be totally abandoned for this activity!

1. Accumulate an old stack of magazines. From the magazines, cut out words that are at least ½" tall. You can do this ahead of time or have kids help you with the cutting as a separate activity.

2. Provide everyone with a sheet of paper, glue, and markers—which may be used ONLY to write one's own name or names of others playing the game. You'll also need a timer from a board game.

3. To begin the activity, spread the cut-out words over a large area on the floor. Explain that everyone is going to make statements or phrases (again, don't worry whether these are actually sentences).

4. Points will be awarded for number of words included in phrases at the end of each timed round. The word count could (or could not) include names of all the participants included in the sentence. These names will be written in marker amid the pasted words. For example (underlining indicates names written with marker):

    <u>Emily</u> is now doing all yard work for **<u>Scott</u>** and **<u>James</u>**.

    Come up with your own rules. You might consider the following: Is criticism of others (or their work) allowed, are the sentences limited in subject area, how often may players use their own name and names of others, are both positive and negative statements allowed?

Pen Pal Package Deal

1. Locate an organization that can provide names of families somewhere across the world who speak one of the same languages your family speaks. Your written skill in the language needs to be sufficient to communicate back and forth either by e-mail or actual letters. Ideally, try to find a family with enough members so that each person in your family has someone with whom to correspond.

2. As a family, discuss what kinds of topics might be interesting to your pen pal family. Together, look for events and experiences that might make for interesting letter material—a festival in your area, a weather phenomena, a home repair project, a school play, etc. Encourage kids to emphasize events and ideas (what kind of music they like, for example) rather than material acquisitions (what CD they just bought). Think of questions to ask that, while not overly personal, will give your family an idea of what life is like in your pen pals' country.

3. As simultaneous letters are generated back and forth, they will provide an emerging picture of another family's daily life as well as conversation for your family on something you'll all have in common. You might even read different versions of the same event from different family members, an occurrence that may lead you to wonder if your pen pal family is having the same experience reading your letters.

Nursing Home Narrations

Here's a volunteer opportunity for all members of your family to participate in together, one that, at the same time, will give you an opportunity to talk with your kids about the lives of older people. You might even be able to organize the activity at a residence where one of your family members lives. Before you start out, if your kids aren't already aware of both the limitations and strengths that they might observe in older people, explain what they might expect from their visits. Here's how to begin:

1. Get permission from the director of the facility to conduct this activity.

2. Visit once to meet the residents and talk about an upcoming holiday. In this case, Valentine's Day is used as an example.

3. Ask residents to relate one specific memory about that holiday; it might be signing penny valentines, receiving a box of chocolate-covered cherries from someone special, the transformation of a high school gym into a Valentine Dance Palace, the first handmade valentine he or she received as a parent, etc. Jot down the memory, read it back, make corrections, and ask the residents to spell their names.

4. At home, type up the memories, each one on a separate sheet of paper. Save and print. Visit a second time, arriving with a batch of valentine stickers. While visiting each resident, read his or her memory aloud. Explain to the resident that you're going to make any necessary corrections or additions to the memory; when it's been revised to the resident's satisfaction, attach a sticker to indicate so. Also, check again to make sure the names are spelled correctly.

5. At home again, revise the memories and then combine them all on two or three pages.

6. Print out the pages (take to a copy shop if you need lots of copies) and make them into booklets. If there are younger children or teenage artists in the family, they might like to make the covers. If not, for the cover just use some red paper on which you've written something like the following:

> Valentine Memories
> Hillcrest Manor
> February 2005

7. Distribute the booklets on your third visit. If you would like to take along some treats, check ahead of time and then go for something like sugar-free non-chocolate cookies or candy, or perhaps some little packages of dried fruit. Try to make your third visit about a week before Valentine's Day since many facilities may have plans for the holiday itself.

Note: By celebrating the memories of the members of the facility, this activity can be wonderfully life-affirming. However, some people may feel rather uncomfortable being around so many old people. After completing this exercise, you may want to have a discussion about what it's like to get old, thoughts of death, etc. And while this may initially seem like a morbid topic of conversation, it is important that family members discuss these issues. After all, they're as much a part of life as having a new child or celebrating the holidays. In order to insure that the conversation doesn't solely dwell on the negative aspects of death and dying, be sure to remember all the wonderful stories the residents at the facility were able to share.

Party Plans

Like the planning part of a vacation, sometimes the actual planning of a party is an integral part of the fun. Make writing party plans an activity in itself. While giving a party can't be done that frequently, planning parties can be an anytime activity, even an in-the-car writing activity when one rider is assigned the role of note-taker.

Here's a list of possible themes for small family parties or a larger gathering that includes family and friends. You might want to start by generating more ideas to add to this list before you begin brainstorming for individual parties, ideas that reflect your family's interests.

Chocolate and More Chocolate

Photo Mania

Bring Your Pets

Cartoon Characters

Ancient Times

Sundaes on Sunday

Treasure Hunt

Johnny Appleseed

Groundhog Day

TV Ads Revised

In the News

Sports Heroes

Techno-Nerd

Making Magic

Music Video

Inside Out, Upside Down Day

After discussing these possible themes, brainstorm ideas. Make sure you include ideas for theme-related invitations, refreshments, games and/or entertainment, prizes and/or favors, decorations, etc.

During the brainstorming, keep in mind that this would be a realistic party the family might actually host, so ideas may need to be tempered with compromise so that the party would appeal to all family members as well as the family budget.

If kids really get into this, you might keep a file on the computer (or in a notebook) to be consulted when it's actually time to give a party.

Perhaps a family holiday gift might be a "gift certificate" good for hosting an actual one of these planned parties sometime later in the year.

Another party-writing idea: do a post-party analysis. Go through the list, talk about what worked and what didn't; write down comments about what you might change if you ever give this kind of party again (or any other party, for that matter).

For a totally different kind of party-planning activity, ask each family member to create a fantasy party, one in which expenses were unlimited. Where would it take place, and just how lavish could it be?

Pre"Historic" Writing Party
(pre e-mail, pre-telephone, pre-fax communication)

This is a special party that deserves a listing all of its own. Spend an evening with your family engaged in the very prehistoric mode of pen-and-paper-only writing activities. Here are some possibilities:

- Check out a book from the library on handwriting analysis; explain that this is an entirely unscientific process but it can still be fun.

- Allow everyone a small sum of money to spend ordering an item from a novelties catalog. Learning to fill out an order form—rather than calling an 800 number or ordering on-line—is a great skill. Perhaps you might want to get a party supply catalog to order some items for one of the parties planned in the previous exercise.

- Write an actual letter to someone. Get out all those odds and ends of stationery. Let everyone choose someone to write. If you can, borrow a postage scale. A good communication skill to practice in letter writing is one that is important in conversation as well: Tell about your own experiences and share your thoughts but also ask the recipient questions to show that you are interested in his or her experiences and thoughts as well.

And a Final Idea:
Find Out More About Writing and Writers

Look for opportunities for you and your child to learn more about writing, such as book signings where real authors discuss their books, young author conferences, creative writing classes, etc.

Possible Solutions for Word-Reduction Challenges:

Challenge A:
Arriving for visit noon February 1. Leaving noon March 31.

Challenge B:
Next year I'll remove backyard oak and plant flowering tree.

Challenge C:
Walk three blocks south from Main to Elm.

Challenge D:
Won decathlon yesterday, broke 21-year county record.

Challenge E:
Delicious, moist brownie recipe calls for yogurt.

Chapter 7

The Right Writer Writes Right . . . er, Make That "Correctly"

Joel: Ah! And here's the chance for you to say that you really *do* know what you are talking about.

Peggy: After that last chapter, I'm not really sure how to take that.

Joel: Oh, come on. This is your area. You've taught writing to thousands of kids. And you should be proud of it. You have a real talent for that.

Peggy: Thanks.

Joel: Many of the activities in the book up to this point reinforce writing skills in subtle ways. But this chapter provides exercises to help boost children's writing skills in specific areas.

Peggy: But they're still fun. Parents can choose one of these activities if they notice their child is having difficulty mastering a particular skill, but they can also just do them for a fun way to practice what they already know.

Joel: Perhaps a word of warning is appropriate here as well.

Peggy: What's that?

Joel: Something that we said earlier but really ought to emphasize. Nothing in this book is going to replace the professionals. Just as we can't promise all family conflict can be solved by working through the exercises in this book, we also can't promise that children will be expert writers after they have done all these activities.

Peggy: I'm glad you said that. In fact, many of these activities don't even involve putting pen to paper. They're just intended to contribute to kids' understanding of language. Although that often translates to better writing, that's not necessarily our ultimate goal.

Joel: Because really, we just want families to have a great time together.

Peggy: Communicating both verbally and with the written word.

And Parts of Speech Are Important Why?

The truth may be that only English teachers and their students are driven to distraction worrying about articles and adverbs, but since it may be your kids doing the worrying (or perhaps the ones not worrying when you think they should be), the following activities may help reinforce some of that grammatical language being tossed around at school.

Norbert the Noun Nerd

Get to know Norbert; he's famous in the world of nouns because he feels annoyed if anything (person, place, or thing—make that any noun) appears with him in a sentence UNLESS it begins with the letter "N." So, haul out the dictionary, and Norbert can become well-known around your house.

You might start by simply leafing through the "N" section of the dictionary looking for nouns beginning with that letter. Then put Norbert and the nouns in sentences together. Think about what Norbert liked, ate, carried, won, etc. For example: "Norbert likes nutmeg" and "Norbert went to Norway."

Once Norbert is a familiar character around your house, you might use him to talk about the difference between concrete and abstract nouns. Norbert will actually allow abstract nouns that don't begin with "N" to be included in sentences with him. For example: "Norbert is known for his friendliness, loyalty, attitude, and enthusiasm."

Note: You may want to replace Norbert with "he" every once in awhile as a way to introduce the word "pronoun" into the conversation. Point out that Norbert is okay with that, but, as usual, he's very particular. He says that if he is going to be written into a story, he must be mentioned by name about fifty percent of the time.

Prepositional Pigs

Prepositions and pigs make for a winning combination. After trying this little exercise, kids will remember not only what those creatures are (the prepositions, that is), but they'll also gain an understanding of what is known as "agreement."

1. To start, turn a sheet of paper horizontally. Working together, write a half dozen pig sentences following the examples below. Make half about plural "pigs" and the other half about a singular "pig." For example:

   The pigs   were friendly.

   The pig   was grumpy.

   As shown, leave an empty space in the middle of the sentence. Next, open the book to the list of prepositions found on page 81.

2. Supply everyone with short strips of paper and ask them to write a bunch of creative four-word prepositional phrases. For example:

   "in the taco salad"

   "under the kitchen cabinets"

   "near the Jersey turnpike"

3. Spread out all the slips of paper and let everyone choose a phrase and set it down in a blank spot in one of the sentences. Start out by reading these just for fun. For example:

   The pigs *under the kitchen cabinets* were grumpy.

   The pig *under the kitchen cabinets* was grumpy.

   Then you'll want to point out that the rest of the sentence doesn't change at all when a prepositional phrase is placed in the middle. (A common writing error: Making the verb agree with the nearest noun. For example: "The plate with the potatoes are on the table.")

Super Bowl Special: Adjectives vs. Adverbs

Before the Super Bowl can take place, players may need to play around with the following instant (and very basic) introduction to adjectives and adverbs. Start by reading these examples:

Strong as an ox

Hard as a rock

Thin as ice

Light as a feather

Sour as a lemon

Sweet as honey

Tall as a giraffe

Flat as a pancake

Brainstorm additional familiar clichés, if desired. Now, look at objects around the room and make up descriptions for them. For example:

shiny as the toaster

cold as the inside of the freezer

hard as the floor

Point out that the first word in every phrase is an adjective. Next, pick out objects in the room and talk about what they do and how they do it. For example:

the carpet wears out slowly

the lamp shines brightly

the microwave cooks rapidly

Point out that the last word in every sentence is an adverb. Once everyone has the basic concept, let the Super Bowl begin.

....

1. Divide into two teams (one-person teams will work). You'll need a small ball as well as a scoring sheet and a pencil.

2. Sitting across from each other at a table, the Adjective Adders (Team A) take on the Adverb Adventurers (Team B).

3. Team A announces a category for Round One (such as animals, movies, food, etc.). A player on Team A rolls a ball across the table to Team B, simultaneously calling out a verb.

   Example: "moved"

4. A player on Team B must shoot the ball back while adding an "ly" adverb.

   Example: "moved slowly"

5. A player on Team A rolls the ball back, adding a noun as the subject.

   Example: "The aardvark moved slowly."

6. A player on Team B sends the ball back with an adjective added.

   Example: "The ugly aardvark moved slowly."

   To recap, the order of play is as follows: verb, adverb, noun, and then adjective.

7. Award points at the end of each completed round. Team B (the one supplying the adverbs and adjectives) receives a point for successful completion of the round. For Round Two, play reverses, and the category changes.

Note: You might want to use a timer and penalize for "holding the ball."

Vivid Verbs

Beginners' writing often suffers from an overuse of adverbs. So now that you've played with some "ly" adverbs (in the previous exercise), here's a little activity that demonstrates how those adverbs may be unnecessary if you find, instead, exactly the right verb. Take a look at the following:

OKAY: The horse ran quickly

BETTER: The horse trotted.

Ask family members to describe the way in which they approach various places or activities and then play with possible substitutions for a single verb rather than a verb and an adverb. For example:

"I sprinted (instead of 'ran quickly') to the swimming pool."

"I clench (instead of 'hold tightly') the strap buckling me into the roller coaster seat."

You might also point out the use of these "vivid verbs" in books you are reading together or in newspaper articles. This is also a great time to introduce kids to the thesaurus—with the caution that words have shades of meaning, so it's best to stick with words you've already heard of but just couldn't think up at the moment.

Who Invented Punctuation Anyway?

Even the most seasoned writer would like an answer to that question at times because the rules often seem arbitrary. Here are some short activities that will at least give everybody a chance to review just a few of the basics.

How Does This End?

Challenge everyone to write three- or four-word sentences that can be read in three ways depending on the end punctuation. Here are some examples:

Stop bothering me.

Stop bothering me!

Stop bothering me?

It's fun to exchange these and see what kind of inflection is needed when the reader says them out loud. Here are a few other examples to get you started:

Anybody can do that.

Give me a chance.

Vacuum the rug.

You're not going.

Note: You don't really need to point out the names of the sentence types, but in case it comes up, here's a brief review. A declarative sentence (a statement that makes a fact) ends with a period; so does an imperative sentence (a statement that tells someone to do something). However, an exclamation mark can turn either of those two into an exclamatory sentence. A question mark indicates an interrogative sentence.

Quotation of the Day

For this activity, if you don't already have one, you might like to pick up a book of quotations suitable for all ages. Ask each family member—perhaps once each week or every other week, depending on how many members of your family will share this task—to pick out a quote either from the book of quotations or perhaps one from a book they've been reading.

Next, the quote-finder will copy the quote—either by hand or by printing it out from the computer (complete with quotation marks)—and display it somewhere like the fridge or the kitchen table where it can be read by all.

The point of the activity is twofold:

1. To use quotation marks and make sure the quote-finder realizes that the end punctuation usually goes inside the quotation marks, and

2. To reinforce the idea that quotations must be quoted exactly—word for word, dot for dot, and with quotation marks around them.

You will also have the opportunity to reinforce the term "attribution"—the idea that the speaker or writer always gets credit. The name of the author should appear with the quote. The bonus in this activity comes, of course, from any discussion that the quote might generate.

Comma Confusion

Commas really ought to be teardrop-shaped for all the agony they cause; experts argue endlessly over their correct usage. However, one of the best reasons for using a comma is simply for the purpose of avoiding confusion. Here's an example:

The second grade teacher said the student is thirty-four-years old.

That's a long time to spend in second grade! Add commas after teacher and student, and you get a completely different sentence with a different meaning:

The second grade teacher, said the student, is thirty-four years old.

After working together as a family to sweep away confusion in the following sentences, be on the lookout for misunderstandings caused by missing and misplaced commas on road signs, menus, advertisements, etc.

1. As the trapeze artist on the high wire made her way across the crowd cried out in fear. (Add one comma for clarity.)

2. The box contained tools for carving heads of broken dolls, and yarn for knitting. (Add one comma for clarity.)

3. Many students I know have too much homework. (Add two commas to change the meaning of the sentence.)

4. I don't know Tom when the movie begins. (Add two commas for clarity.)

5. With the stubborn teamwork is often impossible. (Add one comma for clarity.)

6. I told the real story to no one but Jack probably did. (Add one comma for clarity.)

7. Annie left him convinced he was not a good person. (Add one comma to change the meaning of the sentence.)

8. The three most popular items on the menu are sandwiches made with peanut butter and jelly macraroni and cheese and pizza. (Add two commas for clarity.)

9. To Holly Shakespeare seemed difficult to read. (Add one comma for clarity.)

10. When the actor called Sadie an important director and a famous writer were sitting in the room and watching the first scene. (Add one comma for clarity.)

11. On the subject of eating people have many different opinions. (Add one comma for clarity.)

12. Most bats you see are nocturnal. (Add two commas to change the meaning of the sentence.)

Answers for Comma Confusion

Insert commas after the following words:

1. across
2. carving
3. students & know
4. know & Tom
5. stubborn
6. one
7. him
8. jelly & cheese
9. Holly
10. Sadie
11. eating
12. bats & see

It's (or is it "Its?") True: Apostrophes May Disappear

It's true. Even as the use of an apostrophe to show what belongs to whom (the elephant's trunk, as an example), there are those who think that use of the apostrophe may actually be eliminated someday soon—to the great relief of confused writers everywhere.

Meanwhile, here's an apostrophe game that will quickly ingrain the idea of apostrophes as contractions into the heads of all family members who need that kind of review. The activity is called "The Game of Its."

To prepare the game, first write the following sentences on index cards (or type them up and print out onto cardstock, which you can then cut into squares).

That clock is hard to read because ITS hands are small.

ITS raining.

I do not like the storm, especially ITS raining sound.

I'm happy that ITS going to snow tonight.

ITS delicious.

Do you know what ITS made of?

ITS too late.

Before I eat the banana, I'll put ITS peel in the trash.

I'm sorry that ITS broken.

ITS almost 10:00.

Also, make some large, bright-colored apostrophes. Again, you can either manufacture these by hand (kids may enjoy making them) or use a large point size and print them out.

Now you're ready to play. Place the cards facedown between two players. Player A turns the top card over and puts it down on the table. To win that card, Player B must do one of two things.

1. Slap an apostrophe right onto that card—if one is needed, or

2. Grab the card if no apostrophe is needed.

Next, Player B turns the card over, and Player A takes a turn. Players keep all the cards they gather from making correct decisions, and when the cards are gone, the player who has collected the most cards is the winner.

Players may challenge each other's decisions. Figuring out who's right is easy: If the sentence sounds fine when "It is" is substituted for "It's," then it needs its apostrophe!

Organize That!

One of the most valuable writing skills is the ability to organize. As kids learn about topic sentences at school, they'll be expected to understand that (nonfiction) writing is expected to be orderly. Seeing the overview and then the details in descending order—an absolute must for good writing—is a skill that can be learned at a very young age. Following are some organizational activities in age-appropriate order.

The Imaginary Toy Shelf

A beginning reader should be able to take on the following activity. The list below is just a suggestion; you might want to come up with your own lists that include items your child enjoys:

Crayons

Teddy bear

Plastic dinosaur

Sock monkey

Stuffed tiger

Look at the list together and ask the following questions:

Imagine you had a shelf just for your animal collection, which item would not go on the shelf?

What name would you give for the shelf on which you'll keep your crayons?

The next step might be to make a copy of the list and cut the items apart. Shuffle the strips of paper and ask your child to organize them. The ideal arrangement, of course, would be two separate shelves (categories) with the items correctly placed on each.

Put THIS in Order!

Once this sorting process is understood, many kids love making their own cut-up organizational puzzles that they can then ask other family members to reconstruct. You'll want to suggest some topics that are general knowledge for all family members (some possible categories: relatives, types of foods, kinds of movies, etc.)

Organization: Challenge Level

Here are some more advanced puzzles that families might like to work out together. If a puzzle seems too difficult to solve by just looking at the words in the book, you might want to copy the list so that words can be crossed off as you work. An even easier method, of course, would be to cut the words apart and use a hands-on approach.

Organize each of the following lists into an outline that has a main topic, categories that fall under that topic, and the items that would fall under each category:

List 1: taxis, air vehicles, kayaks, dump trucks, rowboats, transportation vehicles, vans, cruise ships, minibikes, railroad trains, hot air balloons, water vehicles, gondolas, jets, motorcycles, buses, helicopters, steamships, land vehicles

List 2: Alligator, birds, turtle, eagle, elephant, snake, animals, horse, ostrich, reptiles, mammals, ant, eel, blue jay, trout, whale, insects, beetle, shark, fish, dragonfly, camel, lion, salmon, dog

List 3: Statue of Liberty, American landmarks, Big Ben, famous landmarks, Golden Gate Bridge, foreign landmarks, Washington Monument, Eiffel Tower, Asian landmarks, European landmarks, Great Wall of China, Empire State Building

Answers for Challenge Level

List 1:

Transportation vehicles
  land vehicles
    taxis
    dump trucks
    vans
    minibikes
    railroad trains
    motorcycles
    buses
  water vehicles
    kayaks
    rowboats
    cruise ships
    gondolas
    steamships
  air vehicles
    hot air balloons
    jets
    helicopters

List 2:

Animals
  birds
    eagle
    ostrich
    blue jay
  reptiles
    alligator
    turtle
    snake
  mammals
    camel
    lion
    dog
    elephant
    horse
    whale
  insects
    ant
    beetle
    dragonfly
  fish
    eel
    salmon
    shark
    trout

List 3:

Famous landmarks
  American landmarks
    Statue of Liberty
    Golden Gate Bridge
    Washington Monument
    Empire State Building
  Foreign landmarks
    European landmarks
      Eiffel Tower
      Big Ben
    Asian landmarks
      Great Wall of China

Syl·lab·i·ca·tion

An easy way to help kids with an understanding of syllabication is to limit the number of syllables included in a story you write together to just one per word! Think of it as if you were writing for a small child or beginning reader. (The stories you write will sound something like an Easy Reader!) Here's an example: Joe wants a treat. He wants cake. The cake is good.

Now, here's the point: You often can't write in past tense. Joe can't have wanted the cake yesterday because "wanted" is two syllables; Joe can't want a cookie instead of a cake because "cookie" contains two syllables. And the cake certainly can't be the three-syllabled "chocolate."

For the next challenge, write a new story, making sure it contains at least two two-syllable words, three three-syllable words, four four-syllable words, and so on, depending on the skill level of the writer.

You might also want to try an all two-syllable story, a challenge because you'll be short on articles (no "a's" or "the's"). Here's an example: Tanya wanted seven orange pencils because other students didn't possess any pencils colored orange.

This activity provides another reason for learning how to use a thesaurus; kids enjoy looking up synonyms for words that contain a different number of syllables. For example, exchanging the one-syllable "own" for the two-syllable "possess."

Epilogue

. . . .

Joel: I always dread this part.

Peggy: What part?

Joel: The part where I have to say goodbye.

Peggy: I thought I was the one who always got all weepy.

Joel: Well, I always know I'm going to see you again. Oddly enough, it's sometimes been more difficult to say goodbye to families I've worked with in therapy.

Peggy: Why?

Joel: After spending so much time with people, getting to know them, and forming a relationship, it's tough to finally say that you have nothing more to offer.

Peggy: But it must feel good to know that you've helped them.

Joel: Absolutely. I guess you probably feel the same sort of pride and sadness when your students graduate.

Peggy: I was afraid you were going to mention that.

Joel: Don't get all sniffly on me now. We've got to wrap this up.

Peggy: I know. I just hope we've done a good job.

Joel: What do you mean?

Peggy: I hope that we haven't misled anyone.

Joel: I thought we were really clear in the last chapter that nothing in this book is going to turn kids into expert writers, and we can't solve all family communication problems.

Peggy: But it's more than that. I don't want to give the impression that this is all about writing. Things like incorrect spelling, poor handwriting, improper grammar—those things shouldn't matter when families do these activities. Kids should be reinforced for their ideas and communicating them effectively. That's what's important. Having good writing skills is great, but there are things in life that are even more important.

Joel: Like having a good time.

Peggy: Would that really be at the top of your list?

Joel: I don't know. It just popped out.

Peggy: Well, if we're talking about important things, I'd have to rate "caring for each other" near the top of my list.

Joel: Then I think we've been successful on both our accounts.

Peggy: How so?

Joel: Everything in this book is designed to help families communicate in a fun and playful manner. And when this happens, they learn to listen to each other's thoughts and respect each other's ideas.

Peggy: I guess we did all right then.

Joel: We did great!

About the Authors

Joel Epstein, Ph.D., is a professor at the Missouri Institute of Mental Health, a division of the University of Missouri's School of Medicine. In 1994, he received the Outstanding Scientist Award from the Missouri Alliance for the Mentally Ill, and was named one of the top 100 multimedia producers by *Multimedia Producer Magazine* in 1996. Joel has taught psychology and multimedia classes and has published numerous academic articles. He lives with his family in Saint Louis, Missouri.

Besides being Joel's mother, **Peggy Epstein** taught English in Missouri and Kansas for twenty-five years. She received her M.A. in Curriculum from the University of Missouri at Kansas City. Peggy is a freelance writer, whose articles and stories have been published in the *Kansas City Star, CollegeBound, Grit, Women's Circle, The Writer, Spider, Ladybug,* and *Footsteps,* among many other publications. In her free time, Peggy enjoys writing musicals with her husband and writing stories with her grandson. She is the author of *Great Ideas for Grandkids* (McGraw-Hill, 2003). Peggy lives in Kansas City, Missouri.